**INTERMEDIATE
ESL VIDEO LIBRARY**

BUSINESSWATCH

Keith Maurice

Susan Stempleski
Series Editor

PRENTICE HALL REGENTS
Englewood Cliffs, New Jersey 07632

Acquisitions Editor: **Nancy Leonhardt**
Manager of Development Services: **Louisa Hellegers**
Development Editor: **Barbara Barysh**
Editorial Production / Design Manager: **Dominick Mosco**
Editorial/Production Supervision: **Jan Sivertsen**
Production Coordinator: **Ray Keating**
Cover Supervisor: **Marianne Frasco**
Cover Photograph: **Comstock**
Interior Design: **Function Thru Form**
Electronic Artists: **Fred Flake**
Technical Support: **Molly Pike Riccardi and Wanda España**

©1994 by PRENTICE HALL REGENTS
Prentice–Hall, Inc.
A Paramount Communications Company
Englewood Cliffs, New Jersey 07632

Video material © 1994 American Broadcasting
Companies, Inc. All rights reserved.

ABC Distribution Company

Printed in the United States of America
10   9   8   7   6   5   4   3   2   1

ISBN 0-13-501164-7

Prentice-Hall International (UK) Limited, *London*
Prentice-Hall of Australia Pty. Limited, *Sydney*
Prentice-Hall Canada Inc., *Toronto*
Prentice-Hall Hispanoamericana, S.A., *Mexico*
Prentice-Hall of India Private Limited, *New Delhi*
Prentice-Hall of Japan, Inc., *Tokyo*
Simon & Schuster Asia Pte, Ltd., *Singapore*
Editora Prentice-Hall do Brasil, Ltda., *Rio de Janeiro*

TABLE OF CONTENTS

ACKNOWLEDGMENTS

Hearty gratitude goes to two TESOLers for their very clear support and assistance: Susan Stempleski, the editor of the "Watch" series, for her superb ideas on text structure and her caring manner. We are very fortunate to have her as an editor.

Frederick L. Jenks, Professor of Education in the Department of Curriculum and Instruction at Florida State University and Director of the Center for Intensive English Studies at Florida State University. His continuing support and advice is invaluable.

I would like to dedicate this text to the three people who fill my life with love: Araya, my wife, who is a full professional and a busy wife, and who also became a single parent on weekends for months while I worked on the text, and Kevin and Bobby Mac, who make me very proud every day for what they do, what they learn, and who they are. You three make it all worthwhile. Thanks.

INTRODUCTION TO THE SERIES

The *ABC News Intermediate ESL Video Library* is an interactive, integrated skills series designed for intermediate level adult learners of English as a second or foreign language. The series consists of five videocassettes: *BusinessWatch, CultureWatch, EarthWatch, HealthWatch,* and *InnovationWatch,* each accompanied by a student text and Instructor's Manual.

THE VIDEOS

Each videocassette consists of twelve actual broadcast segments from ABC News programs such as *World News Tonight, 20/20, The Health Show,* and *Business World.* These authentic television news reports focus on high-interest topics and expose students to natural English, spoken by a wide variety of people from diverse backgrounds and age groups. The videos are time coded and the codes are given in the textbooks so that sequences may be easily identified. The videos are also closed captioned. Teachers who have access to a closed caption decoder may wish to have their students view the captions as they carry out some of the activities. Some suggestions for activities based on closed captions are described at the end of this introduction.

THE BOOKS

Each book offers a broad range of task-based activities centering around the selected video segments. These activities provide practice in all four language skills: listening, speaking, reading, and writing. The reading material parallels or extends the news story and is drawn from several sources. The books also contain complete transcripts of the video segments. The Instructor's Manual, for each book contains an Answer Key to all the activities.

The general aims of the books are:
- To enhance comprehension of each video segment.
- To highlight and exploit specific language on the video.
- To stimulate discussion about the topics presented on the video.
- To offer authentic reading material related to the content of the video.
- To give students practice in writing clear and simple English.

SOME GENERAL SUGGESTIONS FOR TEACHING WITH VIDEO

Only recently has video moved from being something that is switched on and left to present language without the teacher's intervention to becoming a flexible resource for classroom activities. While there is no one "right way" to use video in language teaching, teachers using the materials in the *ABC News Intermediate ESL Video Library* will probably find the following general guidelines helpful:

Familiarize Yourself with the Material. Before presenting a lesson in class, view the entire sequence yourself, preferably several times and with the video transcript in hand. If time allows, try doing the activities yourself, in order to anticipate difficulties or questions your students may have.

Allow for Repeated Viewing. In order to carry out the viewing activities in the lessons efficiently, students will need to see and hear the video sequence and selected portions several times. Each viewing activity in the lessons is accompanied by a time code. Refer to these time codes and then play or replay the indicated section of the video in conjunction with the particular viewing task at hand.

Present Activities to the Students Before Viewing. Students will focus their attention more effectively on the viewing activities if you ensure that they understand the directions for each task before playing or replaying the video sequence.

Get to Know Your Equipment. Practice with the video equipment you will be using in class. The time codes on the video will help you locate the sequence to be shown and any other points you may wish to highlight.

HOW TO USE THE VIDEOS AND THE BOOKS

You can use the news stories in the *ABC News Intermediate ESL Video Library* in the order in which they are presented on the videos and in the books, or you may choose particular video segments according to the interests of your students. The video segments are not graded in terms of grammatical difficulty, and there is no artificial variation in linguistic complexity from lesson to lesson within the books. You can have students work through each exercise in a lesson, or you may choose specific activities to suit your students' needs and particular class schedule.

Each book in the *ABC News Intermediate ESL Video Library* consists of twelve 10-page lessons, each corresponding to a single news segment on the video. Every lesson is structured in the same way and has three main sections: BEFORE YOU WATCH, WHILE YOU WATCH, and AFTER YOU WATCH.

BEFORE YOU WATCH

This section contains previewing activities that prepare students to watch the video by tapping their background knowledge and stimulating interest in the topic. There are three types of activities in this section:

- **Talking Points:** These are questions designed to stimulate general discussion and elicit relevant vocabulary and background knowledge about the topic of the video segment. They also motivate students to watch the video and provide opportunities for them to exchange ideas.

- **Predicting:** These activities encourage students to think about the topic and to predict the kinds of information they think will be included on the video.

- **Key Words:** This is a vocabulary activity to introduce or review words directly related to the topic of the video.

WHILE YOU WATCH

This section contains a variety of viewing activities for students to complete while actually watching the video. The activities promote active viewing and listening and facilitate comprehension by focusing on essential features of the news story. Time codes corresponding to the appropriate section of the video are printed next to each activity. These time codes facilitate access to the relevant part of the video to be played or replayed in conjunction with the particular viewing task.

- **Getting the Main Idea:** This is a global viewing activity in which students watch the entire video segment and answer questions about key ideas (the who, what, where, why, when, and how) of the segment.

The remaining activities in the WHILE YOU WATCH section take students through the video bit by bit to focus on more specific information. In order to carry out these activities efficiently students are asked to watch and hear particularly relevant sections of the video again to gain a detailed understanding of the news story. The activities used and the order in which they are presented vary, but they include a combination of several of the following types:

- **Checking Your Predictions:** Students watch the video and check to see if their predictions about the content of the video were correct.

- **What's Missing?:** This is a listening cloze. Students listen to a portion of the video segment and fill in the missing words in a section of the video transcript.

- **True or False?:** Students watch a section of the video and indicate whether the statements in the exercise are true or false. Students are additionally challenged by being asked to change the false sentences to make them true.

- **Checking What You Hear:** Students watch the video and check particular details that are mentioned on the video.

- **Listening for Details:** Students watch the video and circle the correct answers to a series of multiple-choice type questions.

- **Checking What You See:** This activity encourages students to pay close attention to visual information presented on the video. Students watch the video and check the images they actually see.

- **Notetaking:** Students watch the video and take brief notes on the answers to a series of *Wh-* questions focusing on specific details.

- **Information Match:** This is a matching exercise. Students watch the video and match the names of people, places, or things with related information.

- **Putting Events in Order:** This is a sequencing activity. Students watch the video segment and number a series of events in the order in which they are presented on the video.

- **Making Inferences:** Students watch the video and are asked to reach logical conclusions, based on the facts presented in the news story.

- **Identifying What You See:** Students watch selected portions of the video and identify what they see by writing a brief description.

- **Making True Sentences:** This is a matching exercise in which students write true sentences about the video by combining sentence stems and endings.

- **Who's Who?:** Students watch the video and check the sentences that apply to different people who are interviewed or shown on the video.

AFTER YOU WATCH

This section contains postviewing activities related to the topic of the video. The activities stimulate language use and encourage students to integrate information from the video. This section always contains the following six activity types:

- **Language Point:** In this activity, a selected language function or grammar point from the video is highlighted for further practice.

- **Vocabulary Check:** This activity reviews idioms, colloquial expressions, and other words or phrases used on the video.

- **Discussion:** These are questions that encourage students to relate the information on the video to their own lives and/or the situation in their own countries.

- **Role Play:** This activity provides students with an opportunity to use the information and language they have acquired while working on the video in a freer practice stage.

- **Reading:** This activity offers authentic reading material — such as magazine articles — related to the content of the video.

- **Writing:** In these activities, students are encouraged to integrate and use information from the video to prepare letters, short news articles, and other original documents.

SOME SUGGESTIONS FOR USING CLOSED CAPTIONS

As mentioned above, an additional feature of the videos in the *ABC News Intermediate ESL Video Library* is that all the video segments, with the exception of those from *The Health Show* and *Business World*, are closed captioned. If you have access to a closed captioned decoder (or a television with the new decoder chip) you may wish to open up the captions and have your students do the following variations of some of the activity types in the books:

- **Key Words:** Have students read the captions and call out "Stop!" when they see one of the key words in the captions. Use the pause button to stop the video at that point, and have students suggest the meaning of the word as it is used in the segment.

- **Checking Your Predictions:** Instead of having students *listen for* the information which they have predicted, they can be asked to *read* the captions to locate the relevant information.

- **What's Missing?:** As a variation of this activity, students can be asked to fill in the blanks (using any words that make sense) *before* watching the video. Students then watch the video, and read the captions to check their answers.

- **Vocabulary Check:** As in the variation of the Key Words activity just described, students can be asked to read the captions and indicate when they *see* the idioms, colloquial expressions, and other words or phrases highlighted in the Vocabulary Check.

These are just a few ways in which the closed captions on the segments can be used to enhance language learning. Allow your imagination to come up with ideas. In situations in which a closed caption decoder is not available, students can carry out similar activities by using the video transcripts in the back of the book.

SUGGESTIONS FOR STUDENTS WORKING WITHOUT A TEACHER

Language learners differ from one another in many ways. If you are learning English without a teacher, you should use the materials in the *ABC News Intermediate ESL Video Library* in the way that is most suitable to *you* and *your* situation. However, your work will probably be more pleasant and productive if you do the following:

- Follow the plan of each lesson.

- Read the directions to each exercise carefully.

- Use the Answer Key only when you have to — and that should be after you have completed the exercise. The Answer Key is in the Instructor's Manual.

- If an exercise does not have clear-cut answers in the Answer Key, try to do the exercise with another person: a native speaker or someone at your own level of English.

- Use the transcripts of the video segments to study the language used on the video in detail. The transcripts are printed in the back of the book.

- Set realistic goals for yourself as you work on the lessons. As with learning many other things, the key to successful language learning is to do a small amount of work regularly and frequently. If doing one lesson a week is too much, try doing one over two weeks.

- If you have a closed caption decoder, you may find it helpful to follow along with the speakers and read the words on the screen.

Finally, enjoy improving your English with the *ABC News Intermediate ESL Video Library!*

Segment 1
Wal-Mart vs Brattleboro, Vermont

From: Business World, 8/23/92
Begin: 00:34
Length: 4:82
Note: This segment is not closed captioned.

BEFORE YOU WATCH

TALKING POINTS

Work in groups. Discuss your answers to the following questions.

1. How have people's shopping habits changed in the last 20 years where you live? For food, clothes, electronic equipment, etc.

2. What happens when large chain stores move into smaller cities or neighborhoods?

3. If you owned a small store and a large chain store moved into your area, what would you do?

PREDICTING

Based on the title of the video segment and the questions above, what do you think you will see and hear on the video? Write down four items under each of the headings below. Then compare your answers with other students.

SIGHTS	**WORDS**
(things you expect to see)	(words you expect to hear)

1. _____   _____

2. _____   _____

3. _____   _____

4. _____   _____

KEY WORDS

The *italicized* words will help you understand the video. Study the definitions. The use each word or phrase in a sentence of your own.

1. *Goliath:* a giant champion who was killed by a small man named David; in business, a very large corporation.

   _____

   _____

2. *retailing:* the type of business which sells things to consumers, usually for personal use, for example, department stores, supermarkets, etc.

   _____

   _____

3. *expansion:* the action of making something larger. For example, a business might expand overseas.

   _____

   _____

4. *tax revenue:* the money, or revenue, a government receives through taxes from businesses and individuals.

   _____

   _____

5. *leakage:* loss of business income because of competition. Another way of saying this is that one store's business comes 'at the expense of' another. The second store in this case suffers from leakage.

   _____

   _____

6. *impact:* the effect of one thing on another.

   _____

   _____

7. *super discount stores:* very large stores that sell things for very low prices.

   _____

   _____

8. *exception:* the situation for which normal rules or tendencies do not fit. For example, David was a small man who defeated the giant Goliath. David was an exception to the rule that giants usually win.

_____

_____

WHILE YOU WATCH

GETTING THE MAIN IDEA

Watch the news report and listen for the answers to the following questions. Take brief notes on the answers. Then compare your answers with those of another student.

00:52–05:09

> **What** is Wal-Mart doing? **Where**?
> **Why** do local businesses see this as a problem?
> **How** are local businesses dealing with the situation?

What?	
Where?	
Why?	
How?	

CHECKING YOUR PREDICTIONS

Look at the lists you made in the PREDICTING exercise on page 1. Watch the video and check (✔) the items that you actually see and hear.

00:52–05:09

WHAT'S MISSING?

Listen again to the introduction to the news report. Fill in the missing words.

00:52–01:20

Stephen Aug: The Goliath of (1) _____ , Wal-Mart, the

(2) _____ of the late Sam Walton, founded 30 years ago

this summer, is now the nation's largest retailer. And even the

(3) _____ hasn't slowed its relentless march toward new

stores and higher (4) _____ . One key to Wal-Mart's success

has been its (5) _____ on small and mid-size America, cities

and towns largely ignored by other major chains (6) _____ . But while Wal-Mart's coming may be welcomed by shoppers, it's often the shadow of doom for local (7) _____ that are (8) _____ in its path.

01:20–
02:00

WHAT DO YOU SEE?

Watch the next part of the video with the sound off. Circle the things you see on the video. The first one has been done for you.

1. new car / (pick-up truck)
2. construction workers / Wal-Mart employees
3. lake / river
4. tree-covered mountain / mountain with few trees
5. big city / small town
6. big, wide bridge / small bridge
7. casually dressed shoppers / well-dressed shoppers

01:20–
02:14

TRUE OR FALSE?

Watch the video again. Are the following statements *true* or *false*? Write **T** (true) or **F** (false). Make the false statements true by changing one or two words.

1. _____ Wal-Mart is expanding into the state of Vermont.
2. _____ The town of Brattleboro, Vermont may face added traffic problems.
3. _____ Brattleboro is a new town.
4. _____ According to the Iowa study, 20 percent of Wal-Mart's sales comes at the expense of local businesses.
5. _____ The types of stores hurt the most by Wal-Mart are generally hardware stores, men's clothing stores, and variety stores.

02:15–
04:48

LISTENING FOR DETAILS

Watch the video. Circle the correct answers.

1. What kind of impact has Wal-Mart had on small towns in Iowa?
   a. Little.
   b. Moderate.
   c. Big.

2. What can Wal-Mart's local managers do if a competitor sells something at a lower price than Wal-Mart?

   a. Call headquarters immediately for advice and approval to match the lower price.
   b. Automatically go below the competitor's price.
   c. Automatically match the competitor's price.

3. How many grocery stores in Iowa have gone out of business because of Wal-Mart?

   a. 787.
   b. 887.
   c. 778.

4. What percent of grocery stores does that represent in those towns?

   a. 20%.
   b. 40%.
   c. 60%.

5. What items do supermarkets sell that Wal-Mart also sells?

   a. Fresh meat, fruit and vegetables.
   b. Canned goods and snack foods.
   c. Cleaning supplies, paper products and pet supplies.

6. Why might Brattleboro be the exception to the events in Iowa? (Two answers below are correct)

   a. Because of its local grocery is a food-coop where shoppers are members.
   b Because of many merchants' focus on service.
   c. Because of Wal-Mart's distance from downtown Brattleboro.

7. Which of the following strategies is/are being planned by local businesspeople?

   a. Spending time with customers and providing better service than Wal-Mart can give.
   b. Adjusting hours to match Wal-Mart's hours of doing business.
   c. Both a and b.

8. What advantage does Wal-Mart have in New Hampshire that it would not have in Vermont?

   a. New Hampshire has no sales tax; Vermont has a 5% sales tax.
   b. New Hampshire has more people in neighboring areas than Vermont does.
   c. New Hampshire does not have any Wal-Mart's yet; Vermont already has several Wal-Mart's in neighboring areas.

LANGUAGE POINT: SHOWING UNEXPECTED DIFFERENCE OR OPPOSITION

On the video, the words *but* and *while* are used several times to signal a different or opposite idea. For example, Stephen Aug talks of Wal-Mart's expansion in New Hampshire, then adds "***But*** the nearest community is not in New Hampshire, it's Brattleboro, Vermont.

> ***But***—is usually used with the second part of the statement, e.g.:
> Wal-Mart is expanding in New Hampshire, **but** the nearest . . .

> ***While***—can be used with either the first idea or the second idea, e.g.:
> **While** Wal-Mart is expanding in New Hampshire, the nearest . .
> or
> Wal-Mart is expanding in New Hampshire, **while** . . .

The ideas below are adapted from the video. Match the ideas in column A below with those in column B that show a different or opposing idea of the same topic. Then watch the video to check your answers.

Column A	Column B
1. While Wal-Mart's coming may be welcomed by shoppers,	a. many are relying on customer service instead.
2. While local merchants understand they cannot compete on price,	b. its arrival often means trouble for local business.
3. If you stay above their price, they will leave you alone,	c. but with no sales tax on the New Hampshire side, discounts will be even harder for the Vermont merchants to match.
4. Vermont has a five percent sales tax,	d. but once you go below them, they will go below you automatically.
5. Traffic could become a nightmare,	e. But Brattleboro might prove the exception. The local grocery is a food co-op where shoppers are members.
6. When super discount stores come in, people still buy their groceries at grocery stores, but then buy their non-food items at Wal-Mart.	f. but, of course, traffic is not the only concern.

VOCABULARY CHECK

The words in *italics* are used on the video. Cross out the word that does not have a similar meaning to the word in *italics*.

1. *earnings*	expenses	income	sales
2. *cope with*	adapt to	deal with	benefit from
3. *concern*	problem	convenience	issue
4. *wake-up call*	alert	adjustment	warning
5. *authority*	writer	power	freedom
6. *bank on*	rely on	put money on	depend on
7. *run*	manage	operate	switch
8. *frustrated*	pleased	unhappy	angry

DISCUSSION

Work in groups. Discuss your answers to the following questions.

1. What did you learn about retailing from the video?
2. What are the benefits of big discount retail stores, such as Wal-Mart, moving into an area?
3. What are the drawbacks, or bad points, of such stores moving into an area?
4. How does big business affect smaller businesses in your city? In your country? In the international business world?
5. If you were a small business owner, or manager, in Brattleboro, Vermont, what would you do to compete with Wal-Mart? Be as specific as you can.

ROLE PLAY

Work in groups of three. One student will play the role of the interviewer. The second student will play the role of a local shopper. The third student will play the role of a local businessperson. Read the situation and the role descriptions below and decide who will play each role. After a ten-minute preparation, begin the interview.

THE SITUATION: **A Radio Interview**

Wal-Mart's New Hampshire store has now been open for one year and is doing good business. Many of the local stores in Brattleboro have lost some of their business because of Wal-Mart.

A state-wide TV program called "Vermont Business" has come to the streets of Brattleboro to talk with some local people about the impact of Wal-Mart on the local community.

ROLE DESCRIPTION: **Interviewer**

You are the interviewer for the TV program called "Vermont Business". Prepare a list of questions about Wal-Mart's expansion into the area and its impact on the Brattleboro community. Include some questions for shoppers and some for businesspeople.

ROLE DESCRIPTION: **Local Shopper**

You are a frequent shopper at Wal-Mart. You like the price and selection at Wal-Mart, but wish that the traffic situation could be improved. Be prepared to answer questions about Wal-Mart's impact upon you and upon Brattleboro generally.

ROLE DESCRIPTION: **Local Businessperson**

You own a store in Brattleboro and are concerned about Wal-Mart's success because it hurts your business and hurts many other local businesses as well. If too much business is lost, the local government will lose taxes and the community will not be able to support itself. Be prepared to answer questions about Wal-Mart's impact upon your business, other businesses, and upon Brattleboro generally.

READING

Read the following excerpts from William H. Bolen's retailing text, *Contemporary Retailing*. Then summarize the main points on the chart that follows.

THE RETAILING MIX

As a retailer examines a potential market and those of his or her competitors, an analysis should also be made of various retailing mixes that may be used or are presently being used by stores in the area.

The retailing mix of a store consists of all those elements that make the store the entity it is in the marketplace. It is important to note that a retail store will have a retailing mix. The question is whether it is the best possible mix for the appropriate target market.

The five parts or "P's" of the retailing mix are Product, Place, Promotion, Price, and Personality. By developing the correct mixture of these five elements, the retail store will generally be successful given basic management know-how. The problem with the mix is the appropriate balance of the five elements. If four elements are strong but the fifth is weak, then the whole retailing mix is weak. . . . If one or more . . . are too heavy or too light, the target market may seek out another store. The retailer, then, must continuously juggle the retailing mix to keep it in balance with the target market. It is truly a dynamic concept. . . .

Product

What items are carried in the store—what brands, sizes, colors, how many, and how many other considerations. What services will be offered—home delivery, alterations, credit, interior decorating advice, and so on. Product consists of physical product, if any, plus the various other considerations that are wanted by the target market.

Place

Where is the store or where will it be? In what region of the country should it be located? What town? Should it stand alone or be in a shopping area? Should it be located in the central business district or in an outlying area? Should it be in a conventional shopping center or in a mall? Where should it be in the mall in relation to similar stores? The main stores? Is parking available at the site? Is the area safe particularly for nighttime operations? Is the site accessible to the target market?

Promotion

Promotion consists of advertising, personal selling, and sales promotion. Promotional needs vary with the type of store and the target market it is attempting to reach. A 7-11 type of convenience store may advertise heavily to build traffic but require littel personal selling in the store itself. A clothing store may, on the other hand, require a high level of personal selling to obtain a satisfied customer but require little in-store promotion through point-of-purchase displays as may be needed in a self-service store environment.

Price

Prices influence the target market in many ways. For one, customers tend to equate quality with price. The retailer should, therefore, guard against pricing too far below competition. Such efforts may result in scaring away customers than attracting more prospective buyers. Psychological pricing (41.98 versus $2.00), price lines ($5.00 shirts, $10.00 shirts, $15.00 shirts, instead of 20 different prices between $5.00 and $15.00), and odd pricing (prices that force the salesclerk to make change and give an additional opportunity foR suggestion selling) are three of many pricing alternatives for consideration by the retailer.

Personality

The personality or image of a retail store is an integral part of the retailing mix. It differs from the other "P's," however, in that the other parts of the mix can be changed quite rapidly, but the personality of a store is a long-run concept that is learned by the customer over time. Just as the mention of the name K mart creates a picture of discount and savings, the name Neiman-Marcus engenders an image of high price, high quality, and status.
Neither store would want or desire the personality of the other.

For purposes of definition, the personality of a store is the way in which the store is perceived by the customer. When the customer is away from the store, he or she recalls the store as a total unit and reacts in a positive or negative way to this memory. Personality is, therefore, the result of the total store and all its parts.

What makes or creates the image or personality of a store? Simply put—

everything. Product, Price, Place, and Promotion are naturally integral parts of a store's Personality. The target market of the store itself helps to create the image. The attitude of store personnel can do much to generate a feeling of prestige or bargain basement. It is essential for the store to project an appropriate personality. A confused store image will result in confused customers—a most undesirable situation.

William H. Bolen, *Contemporary Retailing*, 2/E, ©1978, pp.27–29. Reprinted by permission of Prentice-Hall, Inc., Englewood Cliffs, NJ.

MAIN IDEAS:

1. Main problem: _____

2. Continuous challenge: _____

3. List the 5 "P's" of the retailing market and briefly describe each.

   a. **P** _____ _____

   b. **P** _____ _____

   c. **P** _____ _____

   d. **P** _____ _____

   e. **P** _____ _____

4. Essential point about personality: _____

WRITING

Complete one of the following activities.

1. Pick two local stores that sell similar types of items, such as clothing, food, electronic equipment, etc. Compare these stores in terms of the retailing mix, that is, product, place, promotion, price, and personality.

2. Pick one local store and write a brief one-page report on how it can improve its retailing mix. Be specific with your ideas.

Segment 2
New Trends in Retailing

From: Business World, 4/7/91
Begin: 05:20
Length: 5:30
Note: This segment is not closed captioned.

BEFORE YOU WATCH

TALKING POINTS
Work in groups. Discuss your answers to the following questions.

1. What changes, or trends, do you think will occur in the next 10-20 years in shopping patterns? What will cause these changes?

2. How will these changes affect the business world, for example, retailer/manufacturer relationships, employee responsibilities, etc.?

3. What personal characteristics and professional skills will managers need to be able to handle these changes?

PREDICTING
The video is about trends in retailing. Write down your answers to the following questions. Then compare your answers with those of another student.

1. What do you already know about retailing trends?

_____

_____

2. What are you unsure of about retailing trends?

_____

_____

3. What do you expect to learn about retailing trends from the video?

_____

_____

KEY WORDS

The *italicized* words in the sentences below will help you understand the video. Study the sentences. Then match the words with the meanings.

1. *Consumer* spending in the U.S. in 1990 was $1,800,000,000,000.00 retail dollars.

2. The *motto,* "shop til you drop," has been a very popular one for some shoppers.

3. Mercedes has long been considered one of the fine *top of the line* automobiles.

4. Accountants are generally very concerned with the *bottom line.*

5. A married couple with children in school often find that their living expenses keep *mounting.*

6. One of the major *demographic* trends in industrialized countries has been the aging workforce.

7. Many retailers have had to take *drastic* measures to cope with increased competition.

1. _____ *consumer*	a. related to population characteristics
2. _____ *motto*	b. concern with cost or profit
3. _____ *top of the line*	c. increasing
4. _____ *bottom line*	d. quick and severe
5. _____ *mounting*	e. customer
6. _____ *demographic*	f. best
7. _____ *drastic*	g. short expression or proverb

GETTING THE MAIN IDEA

Watch the news report and listen for the answers to the following questions. Take brief notes on the answers. Then compare your answers with those of another student.

05:41–
10:42

> **How** have shopping habits in the U.S. changed?
> **Who** are the business winners?
> **Who** are the business losers?

How?
Who/winners?
Who/losers?

CHECKING WHAT YOU HEAR

Watch the first part of the video. Which items occured before 1990 and which are occurring now? Check the appropriate boxes.

05:41–
07:26

BEFORE   NOW

1. ❑   ❑   "Shop til you drop" echoed through the malls.
2. ❑   ❑   The number of shopping centers rapidly increasing.
3. ❑   ❑   Much empty retail space.
4. ❑   ❑   A "sea change" in shopping habits.
5. ❑   ❑   Nancy Gabriel looking at style as very important.
6. ❑   ❑   Nancy Gabriel looking at price as very important.
7. ❑   ❑   The Gabriels putting additions on the house.
8. ❑   ❑   The Gabriels not putting additions on the house.
9. ❑   ❑   The Gabriels travelling for bargains.
10. ❑   ❑   The Gabriels shopping at discount stores.

NOTETAKING

Watch the next part of the video. Fill in the blanks with the detailed information from the video.

1. What is the typical profit margin of the wholesale membership club? _____

2. What is the typical profit margin of a department store? _____

3. What are three types of shopping that are increasing in popularity?

   _____

   _____

   _____

4. What type of store offers the biggest challenge to typical department stores? _____

5. According to Peter Siris what two things are consumers doing?

   _____

   _____

INFORMATION MATCH

Watch the next part of video. Match the names with the correct information.

   a. BJ's Wholesale Club   b. Cattiva   c. Godfry's   d. Buffams

1. _____ Makes house calls and phones customers after purchases.

2. _____ Has gone, or is getting ready to go, out of business.

3. _____ Now makes dresses that sell for half the price they sold for in the 80's.

4. _____ Is an independent retailer offering extra service to executives.

5. _____ Is a traditional retailer.

6. _____ Is a discounter with a membership concept.

CHECKING YOUR PREDICTIONS

Look at your answers in the PREDICTING exercise on pages 11 and 12. What did you learn about retailing trends? Was it what you expected to learn?

LANGUAGE POINT: COMPARING PAST & PRESENT

On the video, Nancy Gabriel uses *before* and *now* to compare her past with her present when she says, "*Before*, I used to go in, and style or color was a major thing. *Now*, price is really one of the first things I look at."

Change the short passages below, using *before* and *now* as Nancy Gabriel did.

1. While consumers looked toward the top of the line in the 80's, they focus on the bottom line in the 90's.

   _____

   _____

2. Department stores used to be very popular, but giant discounters are more popular these days.

   _____

   _____

3. People have become much more conservative. People are watching what they spend.

   _____

   _____

4. People are watching for investment clothing rather than following fads.

   _____

   _____

5. People are less inclined to buy on impulse than they did in the 80's.

   _____

   _____

6. Having someone meet you at the front door and making sure you get treated properly in the store, make sure the clothes fit you properly, those days are disappearing.

   _____

   _____

VOCABULARY CHECK

The words and phrases below are used on the video. Put each word or phrase into the appropriate category on the chart.

style	retail	catalog	color	glitzy	fancy
wholesale	price	no-frills	outlet	service	margin
turnover	volume				

Shopping Criteria	Store Appearance	Sales & Profit Terms	Types of Shopping
_____	_____	_____	_____
_____	_____	_____	_____
_____	_____	_____	_____
_____			_____

WORD FORMS

The sentences below are from the video. The words in *italics* are either verbs or nouns describing people or actions. Fill in the chart below by adding the other forms of each word. In some categories, there is more than one possibility. Use a dictionary, if necessary. The first one has been done for you. When you finish, compare your chart with another student.

1. The motto, "*shop* til you drop, " echoed through the mall.

2. The engine that drives the American economy is *consumer* spending.

3. In 1990, American consumers spent $1.8 trillion *retail* dollars.

4. Giant *discounters* sometimes sell one type of item like office supplies.

5. People will spend less and will *trade* down if necessary.

6. People are watching for *investment* clothing.

7. Catalog *sales*, television shopping, and shopping by computer are all gaining in popularity.

NOUN DESCRIBING PERSON	VERB	NOUN DESCRIBING ACTION
shopper	shop	*shopping*
consumer		
		retail, retailing
discounter		
	trade	
		investment
		sales

DISCUSSION

Work in groups. Discuss your answers to the following questions.

1. How is each of the following types of business is doing in your homecountry now?

    a. Traditional department stores

    b. Discount stores, e.g., Wal-Mart

    c. Specialty stores, e.g. home appliances

    d. Specialty discount stores, e.g., Toys R Us

    e. Shopping by catalog/mail order

    f. Television shopping, e.g. special programs for shoppers

    g. Shopping by computer

    h. Manufacturer's outlet stores

    i. Other _____

2. How do you think each type of business will be doing in 10 years?

3. How do you think each type of business will be doing in 20 years?

4. Think ahead 50 years. What changes do you think will happen in that time for shoppers and businesses that cater to shoppers?

ROLE PLAY

Work in pairs. One student will play the role of a retail salesperson. The other student will play the role of customer. Design your own role play by matching one of the product categories below with one of the approaches to playing the roles. After choosing the category and your approach, and taking ten minutes to prepare, begin your role play.

Product Category

1. Clothing
2. Home electronic equipment
3. Office equipment
4. Your choice

Role Play Approach

a. excellent salesperson, tough customer
b. terrible salesperson, tough customer
c. funny salesperson, rich customer
d. your choice

ROLE PLAY FOLLOW-UP

After the role play exercise, discuss the characteristics of good and bad salespeople and customers.

READING

Read the following excerpt from Philip Kotler's classic marketing text, *Marketing Management* in order to learn more about retailing trends and to prepare for the final writing task. Complete the matching exercise that follows.

TRENDS IN RETAILING

At this point, we can summarize the main developments that retailers have to take into account as they plan their competitive strategies:

1. **New retail forms.** New retail forms constantly emerge to threaten established retail forms. A New York bank will deliver money to the customer's office or home. Adelphi College offers "commuter train classroom education" in which businesspeople commuting between Long Island and Manhattan can earn credits toward an M.B.A. American Bakeries started Hippopotamus Food Stores to allow customers to buy institutional-sized packages at savings of 10 to 30 percent. Domino's Pizza is set up to deliver pizza within thirty minutes anywhere in its area. . . .

2. **Shortening retail life cycles.** The life span of new retail forms is shortening because of the innovation speedup.

3. **Nonstore retailing.** Over the past decade, mail-order sales increased at twice the rate of instore sales. The electronic age has significantly increased the possibilities for nonstore retailing. Consumers receive sales orders over their televisions, computers, and telephones to which they can immediately respond by calling a toll-free number.

4. **Increasing intertype competition.** Competition today is increasingly

intertype or between different types of outlets. Thus we see competition between in-store and nonstore retailers. Discount stores, catalog showrooms, and department stores all compete for the same consumers.

5. **Polarity of retailing.** Increasing intertype competition has produced retailers positioning themselves on extreme ends of the number of product lines carried. High profitability and growth have been realized by both mass merchandisers such as K-Mart and specialty stores such as Radio Shack and Toys 'R' Us.

6. **Changing definition of one-stop shopping.** Specialty stores in "malls" are becoming increasingly competitive with large department stores as offering "one-stop shopping."

7. **Growth of vertical marketing systems.** Marketing channels are increasingly becoming professionally managed and programmed. As large corporations extend their control over marketing channels, independent and small stores are being squeezed out.

8. **Portfolio approach.** Retail organizations are increasingly designing and launching new store formats targeted to different lifestyle groups. They are not sticking to one format such as department stores but are moving into a mix of businesses that appear promising.

9. **Growing importance of retail technology.** Retail technologies are becoming critically important as competitive tools. Progressive retailers are using computers to produce better forecasts, control inventory costs, order electronically from suppliers send electronic mail between stores, and even sell to customers within stores. They are adopting checkout-scanning systems, electronic funds transfer, in-store television, and improved merchandise-handling systems.

Philip Kotler, *Marketing Management: Analysis, Planning, Implementation, and Control*, 6/E, ©1988, pp. 54, 56. Reprinted by permission of Prentice-Hall, Inc., Englewood Cliffs, NJ

Match the development with an appropriate example. Some of the examples are not given in the text.

1. _____ New retail forms
2. _____ Shortening retail life cycles
3. _____ Nonstore retailing
4. _____ Increasing intertype competition
5. _____ Polarity of retailing
6. _____ Changing definition of one-stop shopping.
7. _____ Growth of vertical marketing systems
8. _____ Portfolio approach
9. _____ Growing importance of retail technology

a. K-Mart & Radio Shack
b. department stores & catalogs
c. checkout-scanning systems
d. Adelphi College & Domino's
e. large corporations expanding; small stores shrinking
f. more change more quickly
g. shopping by TV & computer
h. speciality stores in malls
i. lifestyle mix businesses

WRITING

Complete one of the following activities.

1. You are a business consultant. You have been asked by various retail organizations to study the changes they need to make to remain competitive in the next 10 years. Your task is to (1) select the company you will work with, (2) study how it can best plan for the future, and (3) write a concise 200-250 word report recommending changes it should make in the next 10 years to remain competitive. Your choice can be specific, such as an independent electronics store, one kind of fast food restaurant, or a specific mail-order catalog firm, or more general, such as a television shopping network.

2. Some futurists are saying that the computer age will result in people living in 'cocoons' or 'burrowing,' meaning that they will do most of their shopping and many other activities at home on their computers. If that happens, people and cultures could change drastically. Write a 200-250 word report either (a) predicting how lives and cultures would change if that happens, or (b) explaining why it won't happen.

Segment 3
Too Many Tires

From: Business World, 4/8/88
Begin: 10:52
Length: 6:72

BEFORE YOU WATCH

TALKING POINTS

Work in groups. Discuss your answers to the following questions.

1. In your country, what is usually done with old tires that can no longer be used safely on cars and trucks?

2. Make a list of different ways in which old tires could be used.

3. In some places old tires are burned to produce electrical energy. Do you think this is a good idea? Why or why not?

PREDICTING

Work in groups. Based on the title of the news report, write down five questions you think will be answered on the video. Then compare your questions with those of another student.

1. _____

2. _____

3. _____

4. _____

5. _____

KEY WORDS

The *italicized* words will help you understand the video. Study the definitions. Then use each word or phrase in a sentence of your own.

1. *commercial:* a TV or radio advertisement.

   _____

   _____

2. *dealership:* a business that is authorized to sell a certain product, such as tires or automobiles.

   _____

   _____

3. *dump:* (v) get rid of something; throw away; (n) a place where rubbish is left, for example, an open ground outside a town.

   _____

   _____

4. *entrepreneur:* a person who starts, organizes and runs a business; this is in contrast to a manager who works for a company.

   _____

   _____

5. *incinerator:* a furnace for burning rubbish.

   _____

   _____

6. *private enterprise:* profit-oriented business. This is sometimes contrasted with government, or public, non-profit organizations.

   _____

   _____

7. *"not in my backyard"* (also called the NIMBY syndrome): the problem that describes the situation of people not wanting something (such as a prison or a dump) to be located near where they live.

   _____

   _____

8. *pollution:* the action of making air, water, or the environment dirty or dangerous to live in or use.

_____

_____

WHILE YOU WATCH

GETTING THE MAIN IDEA

Watch the news report and listen for the answers to the following questions. Take brief notes on the answers. Then compare your answers with those of another student.

11:11–
17:17

> **Who** is doing **what, where**?
> **Why** is this a problem?
> **What** seems to be a solution?
> **Why** isn't this solution used more often?

Who?	
What?	
Where?	
Why/problem?	
What/solution?	
Why/not used?	

CHECKING YOUR PREDICTIONS

Look at the questions you wrote in the PREDICTING exercise on page 21. Watch the video. Which of your questions are answered on the video? What answers are given?

11:11–
17:17

WHAT'S MISSING?

Listen again to Barbara Walters' introduction to the news report. Fill in the missing words.

Barbara Walters: It's probably not on anyone's wish list, but you're about to see what a pile of 40 (1) _____ (2) _____ looks like. And while that sounds like a lot, it's only a (3) _____ of the number of tires Americans have (4) _____ away. Since the time of the Model T, we've discarded 2 (5) _____ tires. We add (6) _____ million more each year and what on (7) _____ are we supposed to do with them? And where on earth? Well, (8) _____ has to worry about these things and around here we've nominated John Stossel.

WHAT DO YOU SEE?

Watch the next part of the video with the *sound off*. Number the following items from 1 to 7 in the order in which you see them. The first one has been done for you. (You may need to watch the video several times.)

  _1_ A pick-up truck moving in the desert.

  _____ A mechanic taking a tire off a vehicle.

  _____ The reporter talking to a truckstop worker.

  _____ Large "flocks" of birds flying over a garbage dump.

  _____ A pick-up truck moving in the snow.

  _____ Garbage being moved at a garbage dump.

  _____ A couple of tires being dumped in back of a gas station.

NOTETAKING

Watch the next part of the video and take brief notes on the answers to the following questions. Then compare your notes with those of another student. (You may need to watch the video several times to complete the exercise.)

1. What do gas stations do with old tires?

   _____

2. What don't gas stations take the old tires to dumps?

   _____

3. What is one danger of tires being left in stockpiles?

_____

4. What do some companies do with old tires?

_____

5. How much does the rancher in Modesto, California get for each tire he collects?

_____

6. How many tires are in the pile on the land owned by the rancher?

_____

7. Why was John Stossel a little nervous about walking around the pile?

_____

8. What are some people going to do with the tires in the pile?

_____

9. How many homes will this affect?

_____

10. What can one tire do for one home each day?

_____

TRUE OR FALSE?

Watch the next part of the video. Are the following statements *true* or *false*? Write **T** (true) or **F** (false). Make the false statements true by changing one or two words.

15:51–
17:05

1. _____ Each tire is equal to 20 gallons of oil.
2. _____ The tires can be transformed into electrical energy.
3. _____ Many cities and communities all over the country want these kinds of energy factories.
4. _____ The factory produces a bad smell.
5. _____ Half the plant consists of pollution control equipment.
6. _____ The equipment has been used in Germany for 40 years.
7. _____ The equipment has been tested in California and the air is clean.
8. _____ A similar plant is being built in New Hampshire because the local people want it.

LANGUAGE POINT: PASSIVE VOICE

On the video, John Stossel uses the passive voice when he says, "It makes sense: tires *are made* from oil." Complete the paragraphs below with the passive form of the verbs in parentheses. The first one has been done for you.

Over 200 million tires *are discarded* by Americans each year. When
(1. discard)

a tire _____ away, it usually ends up in a pile behind a gas
(2. throw)

station. Unlike paper trash, which decomposes rather quickly when it

_____ to sun and water, rubber takes hundreds of years to
(3. expose)

disintegrate. Some people try to hide old tires by burying them. However

this doesn't work because when tires _____ , they usually
(4. bury)

return to the surface.

Entrepreneurs have suggested other solutions to the problem. In

Massachusetts, pieces of old tires _____ to make fishing nets. In
(5. use)

Minnesota, tires _____ into a powder that _____ to make
(6. convert)   (7. use)

carpet backing and hockey pucks. In California, there is a plan to burn

tires and transform the rubber into electrical energy. Until such practical

plans _____ across the nation, the garbage problem will only
(8. adopt)

become worse.

VOCABULARY CHECK: IDIOMS

The following sentences are from the video. What do the idioms in *italics* mean? Circle the answer that is closest in meaning.

1. They look so good in the commercials but it doesn't take long before you're at some tire dealership or gas station saying, *"Take it off. I need a new one."*
   a. throw it away
   b. remove it
   c. burn it up

2. So, most gas stations around the country *end up with* piles of used tires like this one.
   a. throw away
   b. receive and keep
   c. finish off

3. . . . landfills are *running out of* room and even those that have room don't like tires because, well, tires are forever or almost forever.
   a. using up all their space
   b. moving from one place to another
   c. renting out available space

4. People who just can't find a legitimate way to *get rid of* old tires dump them.
   a. become free of
   b. get a better brand of
   c. trade in

5. Tires *are made from* oil.
   a. are changed into
   b. are produced from
   c. are separated from

6. It's not done here because nobody wants it in their back yard. I mean, we will wallow in our trash before we'll *deal with it*.
   a. negotiate with someone to handle it for us
   b. take the trash to the incinerator
   c. try to solve the problem

7. Half the plant is pollution control equipment. It's been used in Germany for 14 years. Here they just had testing in California, the air is clean. *It works*.
   a. It can be done with much effort
   b. It is effective.
   c. It is being tried out and experimented with

8. They're just about to *give up on* trying to build a plant in New Hampshire, however, because the local people said no.
   a. stop
   b. start
   c. succeed in

DISCUSSION

Work in groups. Discuss your answers to the following questions.

1. What do you think of the solutions offered on the video? Are there better solutions to this problem? If so, what are they?
2. How can and should business people and companies be involved in environmental concerns, such as recycling and waste disposal?
3. Choose one of the four products listed below and think of some creative uses for these items when they are old and discarded. If you have time, prepare some visual aids to illustrate your ideas. Your brainstorming discussion here will help you with the role play.

      aluminum cans   plastic bottles   cars   computers

ROLE PLAY

Work in pairs. One student will play the role of TV interviewer. The other student will play the role of "recycled product planner". Read the situation and role descriptions below and decide who will play each role. After a ten-minute preparation, begin the TV interview.

THE SITUATION: **A TV Interview**

    ABC News "Business World" is doing a special program on *Recycling and the Future* and has invited a product planner to talk about his or her work with recycled products.

ROLE DESCRIPTION: **Interviewer**

    You are the interviewer for "Business World". Prepare a list of questions to ask the product planner about his or her work; the specific products the planner deals with and the creative ideas he or she has for these products.

ROLE DESCRIPTION: **Product Planner**

    You are a product planner whose work involves finding many creative uses for old and discarded products. Be prepared to answer questions about your work and your creative ideas. You are very enthusiastic about your creativity and your planning.

READING

Read the article on the next page and supply the information that is asked for in the notetaking form that follows:

FROM BUSINESS VS. ENVIRONMENT TO GOOD ENVIRONMENTAL BUSINESS?

For many years and in many countries, the problems of the business community have often seemed to be very different from the problems of the environment. To be successful in business often means exploiting the environment in various ways. The more a business makes and sells, the more successful it is. On the other hand, those who try to protect the environment often end up fighting those in business and those who need work to survive. The more a business makes and sells, the more destructive to the earth it can be.

The examples of this conflict are numerous. The lumber industry cuts down trees for construction, development, and material. That creates many jobs and makes our lives more comfortable. However, deforestation, i.e., the mass destruction of forest lands, with all the benefits to the earth that they provide, has become a huge problem in various parts of the world. While the appetite of consumers for lumber products is greater than ever, the supply is decreasing in many places. The automobile industry, one of the symbols of strong industrialized economies, uses many resources to produce its vehicles which then add greatly to the tire dumps seen in the video and to air pollution all over the world. The oil and chemical industries have made life in the modern world much more convenient for people, and yet the damage caused because of leaks, accidents, storage, and pollution are becoming increasingly troublesome. Some industries focusing on the newer technologies, e.g., computer-related products, tend to use and pollute vast amounts of water. The list goes on and on. The business cycle never ends but recycling efforts often have trouble beginning.

The conflict, then, between economic issues and environmental issues is a very real one with many diverse implications for various groups. Can businesses become more environmentally responsible and still prosper financially? If the growth of certain types of business is slowed or stopped, what will happen to the workers affected? Will consumers buy products that are better for the environment? Will consumers pay higher prices, if needed, for products that are better for the environment? Will national governments support free trade with other nations which use lower environmental standards for business?

People need work to survive economically, but ultimately, civilizations need a balanced environment to survive over the long term. One key question, then, for the 1990's and beyond is this: Can ways be found to solve the conflicting needs of economics and environment so that businesses prosper, workers work, and the earth's ecological system remains healthy?

Interestingly enough, many solutions have been known about for a long time, e.g., solar and wind power for energy needs and electric cars for transportation, but have not reached the point of being accepted on a mass basis. Other solutions, such as recycling of aluminum, plastics, and paper, have become widespread in certain areas of the world. Still others have involved the business community in changing the way it does business, e.g., McDonald's reducing its use of thick containers. And some businesses have developed new processes to deal with trash. One example is Thomas Ceramic, in Japan, which turns garbage into superhard ceramic bricks for construction.

If the business community generally, and hardworking entrepreneurs specifically, respond to the challenges of the environment with the same creativity used to face the issues of transportation, communication, and other concerns of the 20th century, we are likely to see changes in the next 20-30 years that seem impossible now.

1. Give the main idea:

   _____

   _____

2. "The more a business makes and sells, the more destructive to the earth it can be." List (4) industries with environmental problems they create that confirm this statement.

INDUSTRY	PROBLEM(S)
a. _____	_____
b. _____	_____
c. _____	_____
d. _____	_____

3. List the implications (as they refer to each item below) that can occur as a result of the conflict between economic issues and the environmental issues.

   a. Business: _____

   b. Workers: _____

   c. Consumers: _____

   d. National governments: _____

4. Give examples of solutions for the following industries:

   a. Power: _____

   b. Transportation: _____

   c. Widespread trend: _____

   d. McDonald's: _____

   e. Thomas Ceramic: _____

WRITING

Complete one of the following activities.

1. Write a clear and concise executive summary, 200-250 words, on what is being done by business companies and governments to recycle or re-use products in your country. Discuss briefly why more should or should not be done. Explain your reasons.

2. Write a clear and concise executive summary, 200-250 words, on the *reasons why* and the *ways how* one particular company, or industry, should do more environmentally.

Segment 4
Disney's Long-Term Strategies

From: Business World, 3/29/92
Begin: 17:27
Length: 6:07
Note: This segment is not closed captioned.

BEFORE YOU WATCH

TALKING POINTS

Work in groups. Discuss your answers to the following questions.

1. What images do you have when you hear the terms, "Disney," Disneyland," "Disneyworld," and "Mickey Mouse"? In your opinion, why are Disney's movies and theme parks so popular?

2. What types of people generally like to go to Disney's movies and theme parks? What types of people generally do not like to go?

3. What are the advantages and disadvantages for a nation or community in attracting a foreign company to build an operation there?

PREDICTING

The video is about Euro Disney. Write down the answers to the following questions. Then compare your answers with those of another student.

1. What do you already know about Euro Disney?

_____

2. What are you unsure of about Euro Disney?

_____

3. What do you expect to learn about Euro Disney from the video?

_____

KEY WORDS

The *italicized* words will hep you understand the video. Study the
definitions. Then use each word or phrase in a sentence of your own.

1. *revenues:* the gross income, or money, received from business

   _____

   _____

2. *financing:* the process of getting money for a project

   _____

   _____

3. *equity:* the right of ownership in a property

   _____

   _____

4. *cash flow:* the money remaining after expenses are taken out; this is
   similar to, but not the same as, net income

   _____

   _____

5. *shareholders:* the people or organizations that invest in a company

   _____

   _____

6. *net income:* the money received after all charges, e.g., payroll, taxes,
   are paid

   _____

   _____

7. *incentives:* the actions or offers one makes to persuade someone to
   do something

   _____

   _____

8. *tax break:* a lower tax given to a company, often as an incentive to
   move to or stay in a particular location

   _____

   _____

WHILE YOU WATCH

GETTING THE MAIN IDEA

Watch the new report and listen for the answers to the following questions. Take brief notes on the answers. Then compare your answers with those of another student.

17:43–
23:26

> **Who** is building **what, where**?
>
> **How** much will the project cost?
>
> **What** is so unusual about the financing of the project?

Who?	
What?	
Where?	
How much?	
What/unusual?	

IDENTIFYING WHAT YOU SEE

Watch the first part of the video again with the sound off. Match the time codes with the things you see on the video.

18:10–
18:49

1. 18:10-18:14 ___   a. Mickey Mouse clock being moved

2. 18:15-18:17 ___   b. workers painting on top of a building

3. 18:18-18:20 ___   c. pictures of opening day at the original Disneyland

4. 18:20-18:25 ___   d. overhead view of the Euro Disney Park

5. 18:26-18:27 ___   e. workers sweeping the streets

6. 18:28-18:30 ___   f. gardeners working with the greenery

7. 18:37-18:49 ___   g. workers painting a mural on the wall and ceiling

LISTENING FOR DETAILS

Watch the first part of the video again. Circle the correct answers.

1. What Disney movie is mentioned?
   a. Sleeping Beauty.
   b. Beauty and the Beast.
   c. Snow White and the Seven Dwarfs.

2. What does Disney's long-term strategy rely heavily on?
   a. Its movie studios.
   b. Its theme parks.
   c. A balanced mix between movie studios and theme parks.

3. How has recent attendance in Disney's theme parks been?
   a. It's been down.
   b. It's been up.
   c. It's been steady.

4. How many visitors does Disney predict it will have by the end of the year?
   a. 13.5 million.
   b. 12 million.
   c. 11 million.

5. What was the problem when the original Disneyland opened in 1955?
   a. Overcrowding for the first few days; few visitors for months.
   b. Small numbers of visitors the first few days.
   c. Mechanical problems with rides and equipment.

6. How many hotels and hotel rooms are waiting for the visitors?
   a. Five hotels and 6,000 rooms.
   b. Six hotels and 6,000 rooms.
   c. Six hotels and 5,000 rooms.

NOTETAKING

Watch the next part of the video and complete the chart below:

1. The Walt Disney Company of California

Disney's investment	$	
Total investment	$	
Disney's equity		%
Disney's management fee		%
Disney's royalties		%
Disney's cash flow		%

2. List (4) incentives of the French government to Disney:

1. _____

2. _____

3. _____

4. _____

MAKING TRUE SENTENCES

Watch the next part of the video. Then use the chart below to make four true sentences. Write the sentences on the lines that follow.

20:57–
22:28

The labor representative believes . . .	1. . . . that it is unfair for Disney to ask you to take your nose ring out.
One of the job seekers believes . . . Some people believe . . .	2. . . . that Disney will bring "hamburger culture to the land of haute culture. 3. . . . that the French government won the contract at the expense of many
Mr. Fitzpatrick, the Disney executive, does not believe . . .	4. . . . that France is an old lady terrified of a mouse.

1. _____

2. _____

3. _____

4. _____

CHECKING WHAT YOU HEAR

Watch the last part of the video and check (✔) Disney's marketing actions and the analyst's comments that are mentioned.

22:28–
23:13

1. ❏ a store selling souvenirs and t-shirts

2. ❏ a house-sized scale model of the magic kingdom touring Europe

3. ❏ a scale model of Sleeping Beauty's castle touring eastern Europe

4. ❏ heavy advertising in Japan and the U.S.

5. ❏ heavy television coverage all over Europe on the first day

6. ❏ extensive posters and flyers all over Paris

7. ❏ "It's going to be very, very hard for Disney to lose any money on this thing."

CHECKING YOUR PREDICTIONS

Look at your answer to question 3 in the PREDICTING exercise on page 31. What did you learn about Euro Disney from the video? Was it what you expected to learn?

AFTER YOU WATCH

LANGUAGE POINT: DEFENDING A POSITION

On the video, the President of Euro Disney defends Disney's deal by saying, "I think it's important to note that the investment of the Walt Disney Company was by no means a sure thing."

Here are four common ways of defending a position:
a. I think it's important to note that . . .   b. It's important to remember that . . .   c. Please remember that . . .   d. You must realize that . . .

Defend positions based on the following situations. Use expression a, b, c, or d as indicated.

Example: Defend Disney's royalties for the use of the Disney name. (c)

Please remember that the Disney name almost guarantees success.

1. Defend the management fee that the Disney Co. gets. (b)

   _____

2. Defend the French government's incentives to get the project. (c)

   _____

3. Defend the labor representative's criticism that the French government won the contract at the expense of many laws and social rights. (d)

   _____

4. Defend the Disney Company's strict dress and appearance code. (a)

   _____

VOCABULARY CHECK

The words and phrases listed below are used on the video. Put each word or phrase into the appropriate category.

net income   equity   TV coverage   royalties   hard bargain
tax break   stock   investment   incentives   loan guarantees
blitz   threat   bidding war   publicity   management fee

Ownership Terms	Revenue Terms	Government Actions	Marketing Terms	Bargaining Terms
_____	_____	_____	_____	_____
_____	_____	_____	_____	_____
_____	_____	_____	_____	_____

DISCUSSION

Work in groups. Discuss your answers to the following questions.

1. What are the advantages and disadvantages for a company to build a plant in another country?

2. What cultural differences and sensitivities are important for business executives to realize and deal with when working overseas?

3. How much should companies and executives adapt to local business customs and habits when overseas?

ROLE PLAY

Work in threes. One student will play the role of a business executive. The second student will play the role of a business reporter. The third student will play the role of a reporter for a local newspaper. After a ten-minute preparation, begin the press conference.

THE SITUATION: **A Press Conference**

A large multinational company, _____ (name of company) has just built a plant in _____ (name of country). The company's vice-president for international operations has been sent from headquarters to handle certain problems the company has had in this location. Because of various controversial stories in the local newspapers, he has decided to hold a press conference. Reporters have been invited from both local and international media.

ROLE DESCRIPTION: **Company Executive**

You are the vice-president for international operations for _____ , a large multinational company. Be prepared to answer difficult questions and defend your company's performance in using local parts suppliers, promoting local managers within the company, dealing with local employees, and general business plans in the host country.

ROLE DESCRIPTION: **Business Reporter**

You are a business reporter for a weekly international business magazine. You have been following various stories of multinational companies moving into new countries. You are interested in this company's business plans for the future, its local situation, and the possible problems of lower productivity and quality levels at the new plant.

ROLE DESCRIPTION: **Local Reporter**

You are a reporter for a local newspaper which has been very critical of the multinational influence in your country. You want to ask many tough questions of the business executive, especially with what you think is the company's poor performance on working with local suppliers, promoting local managers, treating local workers fairly, and promoting the local economy.

READING

Read the following excerpts from *Weighing Costs and Benefits* by Matthew Lynn, part of a cover story on Japanese industry in Europe in *International Management*. Then answer the questions that follow.

WEIGHING COSTS AND BENEFITS

Japanese manufacturers bring welcome jobs and know-how. But the benefits have to be weighed against the cost to European companies staying competitive.

The motor industry, Europe's largest manufacturing sector, has become a test bed for the impact of Japanese industrialists on Europe.

Nissan decided as long ago as 1984 to build a car plant in the UK. It was swiftly followed by rivals Toyota and Honda. But it has taken until now for the effect to be felt. Last year more than 200,000 cars rolled off the Nissan assembly lines in Sunderland, helping to push the Japanese share of the European car market to 12.3% (1.6 million cars) from 11.7% in 1990. The cars are being made in plants where outputs per worker is twice the European average—hence the shake-out in the industry.

For champions of Japanese investment in Europe this is a sobering thought. The prospect of job creation was a key argument in favor of giving generous subsidies in order to encourage Japanese manufacturers to come to Europe. So far, Japanese carmakers have created 11,775 manufacturing jobs in their European factories in the UK and Spain. More are expected as plants are expanded.

But more may be lost at European carmakers squeezed by Japanese competition. 'It is quite possible there will be a net loss of jobs,' says Mark Cliff, chief economist at the Nomura research institute in London.

. . . The Japanese are simply more productive than the Europeans, partly because they use more advanced manufacturing techniques, and partly because they are starting from scratch on greenfield sites, unencumbered by old plant and traditional attitudes. ...

Big reductions in the labor force are also the price of productivity gains. When Opel, which is owned by General Motors of the U.S., opens its new site near Eisenach, east Germany, it will produce 150,000 cars a year with about 2,000 people. The town's old Wartburg plant employed 9,000 people to turn out fewer than half that number of vehicles. . . .

. . . Workers laid off from car plants are unlikely to find jobs in newer, more productive industries. Many will join the ranks of the long-term unemployed, draining resources from the rest of the economy.

Opponents of Japanese manufacturing investment in Europe claim that their factories are just 'screwdriver' plants assembling components made in Japan. If so, the effect would be to transfer work and wealth out of Europe.

Many of the Japanese manufacturers in Europe are responding to this criticism by increasing 'local content.' Toyota says that when cars start rolling off its new UK assembly lines 60% of the value will be European, rising to 80% by the middle of the decade.

However, the largest survey of Japanese manufacturers in Europe, carried out annually by the Japan External Trade Organization (Jetro), suggests that the screwdriver mentality dies hard. . . . Most manufacturers told Jetro that their local content was staying the same or being reduced. The reason given was poor performance on the part of European suppliers. The upshot is that local content figures are unlikely ever to match those of the European manufacturers being replaced by Japanese competitors.

Not all local suppliers fall short of Japanese expectations. Yoshio Yamaguchi, a director of Mitsubishi, says most Japanese electronics manufacturers in Europe are wrestling with two major tasks: to attain world competitiveness and to enhance local content. But he admits that 'most of the time, those two tasks contradict each other.'

While the job-creating impact of Japanese investment in Europe is open to question, it does have two clear-cut benefits. One is that Japanese investment will reduce Europe's trade imbalance with Japan. The other is that importing more sophisticated manufacturing techniques can be a catalyst for revitalizing moribound European industries. . . .

Adapted and reprinted with permission of *International Management,* excerpts from "Weighing Costs and Benefits" by Matthew Lyon, May, 1992, pp 36-38.

1. List the costs and benefits of Japanese investment in Europe?

COSTS	BENEFITS
_____	_____
_____	_____
_____	_____
_____	_____

2. How do *opponents* of Japanese manufacturing investments in Europe feel about their factories?

_____

_____

3. How do the Japanese manufacturers *in Europe* respond to this?

_____

_____

4. What are the two, often contradictory tasks that Japanese companies need to focus on?

_____

_____

_____

WRITING

Complete one of the following activities.

1. You work for the multinational company _____ (name of company), and you have been asked to prepare an executive summary, 200-250 words, explaining and recommending action to your CEO (Chief Executive Officer) on a site for a new plant. Your executive summary should include (a) the area or areas under consideration, (b) the good and bad points, or pros and cons, of the area(s), and (c) your recommendation on what to do or where to go.

2. You work for a local company that has supplied parts to a local manufacturer that has shut down its plant. A multinational company is preparing to build a factory in your city. Write an executive summary to your CEO (Chief Executive Officer) on what should be done to get the parts business of the multinational. Your executive summary should include (a) the various choices your company has, (b) the pros and cons of each choice, and (c) your recommendation on which choice should be made and how it should be implemented.

Segment 5
The International Airline Industry

From: Business World, 2/23/92
Begin: 23:36
Length: 5:93
Note: This segment is not closed captioned.

BEFORE YOU WATCH

TALKING POINTS

Work in groups. Discuss your answers to the following questions.

1. What do you know about the changes in the international airline industry?

2. What is important to you when you travel by commercial airlines, e.g., safety record, on-time record, service, etc.?

3. What do you think will happen to the airline industry in the next 10 years?

4. Do you think the national flag carriers, that is, airlines that represent their countries, should be maintained even if they are not competitive? Why or why not?

PREDICTING

Work in groups. Based on the title of the news report, write down three questions you think will be answered on the video.

1. _____

2. _____

3. _____

KEY WORDS

The *italicized* words in the sentences below will help you understand the video. Study the sentences. Then match the words with the meanings.

1. The company may go out of business soon. It has filed for *bankruptcy.*

2. The government is trying to let businesses compete on their own; it is moving toward *deregulation* of the industry.

3. Losing one's job is a *traumatic* experience; it hurts for a long time.

4. There has been a *shakeout* recently in the retailing industry.

5. Various companies joined together by *merger* in the 80's.

6. That department is the *sacred cow* in our company; nobody can do anything against it.

7. Small companies sometimes enter into *alliances* in order to become stronger.

8. The government's agricultural *subsidies* to farmers have been very controversial overseas.

1.	_____ *bankruptcy*	a.	the action of two businesses combining; it is similar to the idea of consolidation
2.	_____ *deregulation*	b.	associations or connections between various businesses to further their mutual interests
3.	_____ *traumatic*	c.	something that cannot be criticized easily because of the value it has to others
4.	_____ *shakeout*	d.	government gifts and support to specific industries or companies
5.	_____ *merger*	e.	business failure, with legal implications
6.	_____ *sacred cow*	f.	severely stressful and painful
7.	_____ *alliances*	g.	government action to reduce the rules that businesses must face
8.	_____ *subsidies*	h.	failure of some businesses in an industry

CATEGORIZING TERMS

The words and phrases below are used on the video. Put each word or phrase into one of the categories on the chart.

pooling	join hands	reform
noncompetitive	state-owned	consolidation
demise	failure	national flag carrier

TERMS OF WORKING TOGETHER	TERMS RELATED TO GOVERNMENT	TERMS ABOUT PROBLEMS
_____	_____	_____
_____	_____	_____
_____	_____	_____

WHILE YOU WATCH

GETTING THE MAIN IDEA

Watch the news report and listen for the answers to the following questions. Take brief notes on the answers. Then compare your answers with those of another student.

23:52–29:22

Who is doing **what, where**?

Why are they doing this?

Who?	
What?	
Where?	
Why?	

CHECKING YOUR PREDICTIONS

Look at the questions you wrote in the PREDICTING exercise on page 41. Watch the video again. Which of your questions are answered on the video? What answers are given?

23:52–29:22

WHAT'S MISSING?

Listen again to Forrest Sawyer's introduction to the news report. Fill in the missing words.

23:52–24:27

Forrest Sawyer: Turbulence in the air: this past week the State

Department issued an advisory, warning Americans about

(1) _____ in Europe, the Middle East and Africa. The

(2) _____: possible terrorism in the wake of the latest violence

in the Middle East, another blow just as the airlines were hoping to (3) _____ from a disastrous 1991 brought on by the Gulf war and by recession, and punctuated by the (4) _____ of Pan Am and the (5) _____ of TWA. American carriers hoping to smooth out domestic bumps are turning to (6) _____ routes for profits, but as Stephen Aug reports, there, too, they could be in for a rough ride.

NOTETAKING

24:30–
26:18

Watch the next part of the video and take brief notes on the answers to the following questions. Then compare your notes with those of another student.

1. What four reasons are given for the popularity of European airlines?

   a. _____   c. _____

   b. _____   d. _____

2. What is happening now in the airline industry and how long will it continue?

   _____

3. What U.S. carriers have moved aggressively in the last year?

   _____

4. What two problems do the European airlines face?

   a. _____

   b. _____

5. What is happening among the European carriers?

   _____

INFORMATION MATCH

26:19–
26:35

Watch the next part of the video. Match the airlines with the correct information.

   a. Air France   b. British Air   c. KLM   d. American

1. _____ Is interested in taking over KLM.

2. _____ Is building a terminal gate facility at JFK airport. (two of the above)

3. _____ Is interested in taking over Sabena Airlines. (three of the above)

4. _____ Has gobbled up nearly all of its domestic competitors.

5. _____ Owns 20% of Northwest Airlines.

6. _____ May be shopping for a new European carrier.

7. _____ Has been interested in buying Sabena. (three of the above)

TRUE OR FALSE

Watch this part of the video again. Are the following statements true or false? Write **T** (true) or **F** (false). Make the false statements true by adding one or two words.

26:35–28:23

1. _____ Until recently national flag carriers have been sacred cows.

2. _____ Donald Carty thinks that there will have to be an association if the marketplace is going to work internationally.

3. _____ JFK has been wounded by the demise of Eastern and PanAm.

4. _____ Richard Leone thinks JFK will not survive this fallout.

5. _____ A facility for Luftansa, Japan Air, and Air France is being built on the site of the old Eastern Airline terminal.

6. _____ There may be opportunities for US carriers to join multi national alliances.

7. _____ The partnerships involving Delta Airlines, Swissair, and Singapore Airlines lost money.

8. _____ Nearly everyone agrees that international mergers and industry consolidation are inevitable.

AFTER YOU WATCH

LANGUAGE POINT: GIVING OPINIONS

On the video, Julius Maldutis gives his opinion on the future of the airline industry by saying, "**I believe** that we will end up with perhaps seven or eight global systems operating worldwide."

Here are four common ways of giving an opinion:
a. I believe . . .
b. I think . . .
c. I feel . . .
d. In my opinion . . .

Give opinions based on the following situations. Introduce each opinion with expression a, b, c, or d as indicated.

Example: Give an opinion on the future of the airline industry. (b)

I think that we will end up with about seven global systems and a number of smaller regional systems.

1. Give an opinion on the competition among international airlines. (d)

    _____

2. Give an opinion on the possible loss of national flag carriers, i.e., those carriers that represent and are supported by their national governments. (a)

    _____

3. Give an opinion on the best airlines in the world. (c)

    _____

4. Give an opinion on what will happen to the workers who lose their jobs because of airline failures. (b)

    _____

5. Give an opinion on what will happen to one particular airline in the next five years. (d)

    _____

VOCABULARY CHECK:

The words in italics are used on the video. Cross out the word that does not have a similar meaning to the word in italics.

1. *recession*	depression	bad times	expansion
2. *reliability*	possibility	dependability	consistency
3. *last* (v)	finish	remain	continue
4. *resistance*	opposition	cooperation	fight
5. *wave*	reform	trend	big flow
6. *emerge*	become	fail	rise
7. *take over*	take control of	buy out	join with
8. *inevitable*	destined to occur	unavoidable	inequitable

DISCUSSION

Work in groups. Discuss your answers to the following questions.

1. What did you learn from the video?

2. Do you think it is better for an industry to have more but smaller companies, or to have fewer but larger companies? Why?

3. Besides the airline industry, do you know of any other industries that are moving toward international mergers and industry consolidation? If so, what are they?

ROLE PLAY

Work in threes. One students will play the role of the CEO (Chief Executive Officer) of _____ (name of major company in an industry of your choice). The second student will play the role of Vice-President for Marketing. The third student will play the role of Vice-President for Finance. Read the situation and the role descriptions below and decide who will play each role. After a ten-minute preparation, begin the meeting.

THE SITUATION: **A Strategic Planning Meeting**

The CEO has called a meeting to discuss the situation of the industry and whether the company should move to buy out or merge with another company in order to remain competitive.

ROLE DESCRIPTION: **CEO of _____ (name of company)**

You have called a meeting with two of your closest associates to discuss the possibility of buying or merging with another company in order to remain competitive. You want your company to move ahead, but at the same time, you do not want to risk big losses on a foolish move. Be sure to ask each of your associates the tough questions that need to be answered about any possible decision.

ROLE DESCRIPTION: **Vice-President for Marketing**

You see big opportunities for your company if it moves quickly and strategically to buy out or merge with other companies around the world. You are also afraid of big problems for the company if it does not move quickly. You must persuade both the CEO and the Vice-President for Finance of your ideas, so think carefully about what you want the company to do and how it should go about doing it.

ROLE DESCRIPTION: **Vice-President for Finance**

You have been closely watching the wave of mergers, losses and failures in different industries. You are concerned about the foolishness of some of the executives involved and believe strongly that this company should not repeat the mistakes of others. You think the company should work to reduce costs and that this is a bad time to buy out or merge with another company.

READING

Read the following excerpts from Denise Pelligrini's article, "Dogfight in the Pacific," from Business Tokyo magazine, and then complete the information grid that follows.

DOGFIGHT IN THE PACIFIC

Japanese and U.S. airlines are slugging it out over the world's fastest growing travel market

When bullets started whistling through Beirut in October 1973, sheet-glass salesman Takao Kawasaki grew desperate to get out of town. A loyal Japan Airlines (JAL) customer, Kawasaki was stranded when he missed the final flight to Tokyo. After he spent two nights camped out at Beirut's airport, Pan American World Airways squeezed him on one of its last flights out — and earned his undying gratitude. Twelve years later, he transferred his allegiance to United Airlines when it bought Pan AM's U.S.-Japan routes. Says Kawasaki: "I fly overseas 15 times a year, but unless I'm with my bosses, who tend to favor JAL, I always fly on United."

Loyalty may have brought him to the U.S. carrier, but service is what makes Kawasaki happy with the switch. "The Japanese airlines pamper you too much," he says. "It's annoying. My sleep time on a flight is valuable to me, but on JAL and All Nippon Airways [ANA] they keep waking you up just to ask if everything is OK."

U.S. airlines have decided that picky Japanese customers like Kawasaki are worth wooing. "Right now it is the most important region of the world for us," says William Speicher, senior vice president-Pacific at Chicago-based United.

In their struggle to stay aloft in the recessionary 1990s, airlines around the globe are looking to the Pacific. Growth in North American and European air travel will flatten in the next decade. Asia-Pacific air travel, though, is projected to more than double by 1999, making it the world's fastest-growing region. Yet while demand for seats on Pacific flights is increasing, an acute shortage of flight openings in Tokyo makes it tougher than ever to fill that demand. . . . The shortage of openings in Japan is forcing U.S. airlines to look beyond Tokyo for Pacific hubs. United already has minihubs in Taipei and Seoul and may expand in those cities. St. Paul-based Northwest Airlines, which is competing with United and JAL for top spot among carriers flying U.S.-Japan routes, says it has its eyes on Seoul, Taipei, Honolulu, and Bangkok as hubs.

Still, because Japan will continue to be Asia's biggest air-travel market, foreign airlines will fight tooth and nail to get the slots that materialize. More than 40 carriers without slots at Narita seek openings and most of those who now have some want more. ... The same is true in Osaka, where 20 gates are expected to be built. . . .

Aware that the Transport Ministry will try to give Japanese airlines first crack at the openings, American carriers are lobbying Washington to go to bat for them. The U.S. government may have stood by as Japanese competition devastated American electronics and memory-chip makers, but it will play hardball in protecting U.S. airlines. Air

---

travel revenues are crucial to the U.S. economy. In 1990, U.S. carriers took in $12.9 billion from foreign passengers. More to the point, despite its free-market ideology, Washington is no different from other governments in seeing strong airlines as emblems of national power.

Their plans to expand Pacific routes may be in a holding pattern, but airlines like United and Northwest . . . have begun invading JAL's stronghold by ardently courting Japanese passengers. . . . Northwest has been teaching its American employees how to please Japanese passengers in three-day cultural seminars since last November. In 1991, it spent $500 million to put roomier seats and other amenities on the planes that fly its Pacific routes. . . .

In the same month that Northwest employees started studying Japanese culture, United inaugurated its "connoisseur class" abroad Boing 747-400s. The jets have compact-disk players, Japanese food, and orchids in the restrooms. Having spent $70 million to refurbish its Pacific jets... United is preparing a marketing blitz in Japan. . . .

Japan's Big Two are alarmed at U.S. inroads, but they have other worries to contend with. "Our biggest concern isn't U.S. competitors," says Morris Simoncelli, a JAL spokesman. "It is getting enough pilots." ANA, too, has been hit by a shortage of pilots. Since passenger demand is ballooning, the crunch couldn't come at a worse time. The unions have greeted the obvious solution, hiring foreign pilots, with threats to strike. . . .

U.S. and Japanese airlines may soon be locked in a spending race. Hoping to maximize profits on each of their precious Tokyo slots, they plan to purchase the largest planes available to carry more passengers per flight. . . .

Even if U.S. and Japanese airlines can counter their lack of transpacific slots with better service and bigger planes, industry analysts say they face flak from an unexpected quarter: Asian carriers with weaker unions and lower overhead.

Adapted and reprinted with permission of *Business Tokyo*, "Dogfight in the Pacific" by Pelligrini, February 1992, pp. 28–32.

1. Two adjectives used to describe Takao Kawasaki: _____

   _____

2. The reason that Mr. Kawasaki is glad he switched: _____

3. Projected growth of the following air travel markets:

   North American ____   European ____   Asia-Pacific ____

4. Japanese airport problem: _____

5. Probable government actions:

   Japanese: _____   U.S.: _____

6. Reasons for the actions of both:

   a. _____   b. _____

7. Actions that Northwest and United are taking in the Pacific region:

a. _____   d. _____

b. _____   e. _____

c. _____   f. _____

8. Concerns of Japanese airline executives:

a. _____   d. _____

b. _____   e. _____

c. _____

WRITING

Complete one of the following activities:

1. Research the international airport closest to you and find out:

   a. Which airlines have landing slots or gates and which do not.
   b. How many landing slots or gates each airline has.
   c. How many international flights per day each airline has, both arrivals and departures.
   d. What the government's policy is on granting new slots or gates to airlines.

   After you have done this, write a clear and concise executive summary of the information you have found. (Reminder: Some major international or regional airlines include Aero Mexico, Air Canada, Air France, American, ANA, British Airways, Cathay Pacific, Delta, JAL, KLM, Korean Air, Lufthansa, Northwest, Singapore Air, Swiss Air, Thai Air, and United.)

   (Helpful hint: You can begin your search in the phone book of the city with the airport. or with a local travel agent.)

2. As a consultant to Japan Airlines (JAL), write an executive summary, 200-250 words, advising the CEO what to do about (1) the pilot shortage and union resistance to foreign pilots, (2) competition with U.S. carriers, and (3) competition with lower cost Asian competitors.

Segment 6

North American Free-Trade Agreement

From: Business World, 8/2/92
Begin: 29:33
Length: 5:79
Note: This segment is not closed captioned.

BEFORE YOU WATCH

TALKING POINTS

Work in groups. Discuss your answers to the following questions.

1. What are the advantages of free trade to companies, workers, countries?

2. What are the disadvantages of free trade to companies, workers, countries?

3. Some industries that have been affected by free trade include agriculture, automobiles, computer and communications equipment, and textiles. Do you believe in free trade for all of these industries, some of them, or none of them? Why?

PREDICTING

Work in groups. Based on the title of the news report, predict the kinds of information you think will be included on the video.

1. _____

2. _____

3. _____

KEY WORDS

The *italicized* words will help you understand the video. Study the sentences. Then write your own definition of each word.

1. The *negotiators* for management and the union are trying to hammer out an agreement that will make everyone satisfied.

   negotiators: _____

2. There have been many problems so far. At this point, the *prospect* of an agreement anytime soon is not very good.

   prospect: _____

3. Almost every country uses *trade barriers* to stop or slow down the goods from other countries and to protect local industries.

   trade barriers: _____

4. North American *proponents* of the treaty say that the agreement will help the U.S. economy.

   proponents: _____

5. One concern that many environmentalists have about free trade is the fact that some countries have very *lax standards* on environmental matters. The environmentalists want the standards to be strict.

   lax standards: _____

6. In the last 10-15 years, Japan has had a *trade surplus* with the U.S. while the U.S. has had a trade deficit with Japan.

   trade surplus: _____

7. Some government leaders are concerned about the percentage of *domestic content* in products made by foreign manufacturers.

   domestic content: _____

8. If a country's government raises *tariffs* against foreign goods, it raises the possibility that other governments will do the same to protect their manufacturers.

   tariffs: _____

WHILE YOU WATCH

29:49–
35:05

GETTING THE MAIN IDEA

Watch the news report and listen for the answers to the following questions. Take brief notes on the answers. Then compare your answers with those of another student.

Who is doing **what**, **where**?

Why are some Americans **against** this action?

Why are some Americans **for** it?

What problems are expected for the U.S.?

Who?	
What?	
Where?	
Why/against?	
Why/for?	
What problems?	

CHECKING YOUR PREDICTIONS

Look at your answers to the PREDICTING exercise on page 51. Watch the video again and check (✔) the kinds of information that are actually included on the video.

29:49–
35:05

CHECKING WHAT YOU HEAR

Look at the chart below. Then watch the first part of the video again and check (✔) the appropriate boxes.

29:49–
30:34

How much do these workers earn?	$65 a week	$8 an hour	$0.86 an hour	$1300 a week
Auto workers for Ford in Mexico City				
Auto workers in Detroit				
Solderers for General Dynamics in Mexico				
Solderers in the U.S.				

TRUE OR FALSE?

Watch the next part of the video. Are the following statements *true* or *false*? Write **T** (true) or **F** (false). Make the false statements true by changing one or two words.

1. _____ It's surprising that the prospect of a North American Free Trade Agreement has many in the U.S. worried.

2. _____ Only fools would move manufacturing plants to pay 10 cents in labor for every dollar they are spending now.

3. _____ The Mexican government offered incentives to foreign companies to locate factories in Mexico.

4. _____ Franklin Jacobs, CEO of Falcon Products, says that the Mexican workers are sophisticated and the educational system is fabulous.

5. _____ American critics of the treaty say that if all the trade barriers are torn down, many, many jobs will move south to Mexico.

LISTENING FOR DETAILS

Watch the next part of the video. Circle the correct answers.

1. What did Mexican workers in the Maquiladora program make 10 years ago?
   a. Automobiles and machinery.
   b. Consumer electronics.
   c. Cut-and-sew apparel operations.

2. What products are workers in Maquila making?
   a. Consumer electronics, automobiles.
   b. Parts for military jet planes.
   c. Both a and b.

3. The Institute for International Economics forecasts that by 1995 the treaty will:
   a. Result in a U.S. trade surplus of $9 billion with Mexico.
   b. Result in a U.S. trade deficit of $9 billion with Mexico.
   c. Result in a U.S. trade deficit of only $900 million with Mexico.

4. What do the treaty's proponents say will happen to American jobs?
   a. Some will be gained, and some lost, creating no net gain or loss.
   b. Many will be gained, with a net gain of 130,000 by 1995.
   c. Many will be gained, few will be lost, for a net gain of 230,000.

5. Paula Stern, former Chairperson, U.S. Trade Committee, says that the only growth in U.S. manufacturing jobs has been because of
   a. Exports to Japan.
   b. Exports to Japan and Germany.
   c. Exports to Japan, Germany, and Mexico.

6. Barbara Franklin, Secretary of Commerce, says that the treaty will:
   a. Open a bunch of other Latin American countries for trade.
   b. Open a whole bunch of other Latin American problems for trade.
   c. Open a bunch of expectations that will be too hard to fulfill.

7. Bill Clinton's view on this issue is that:
   a. The U.S. should expand trade with Mexico but not this way.
   b. The U.S. should expand trade with Mexico but needs to be concerned about fairness to American workers.
   c. The U.S. should use its energies to focus on other countries instead of Mexico.

NOTETAKING

Watch the last part of the video. Problems are noted with the treaty, two by Jeff Faux, the labor analyst, two by Stephen Aug, the reporter, and three by John Cregan. List all of them.

33:32
34:55

JEFF FAUX	STEPHEN AUG	JOHN CREGAN
1. _____	1. _____	1. _____
2. _____	2. _____	2. _____
		3. _____

AFTER YOU WATCH

LANGUAGE POINT: PREDICTING

On the video, Stephen Aug reports on other people predicting the future effects of the treaty when he says, "proponents of the treaty say lifting trade barriers *will ultimately* create more U.S. jobs, through increased exports. This study . . . finds that the U.S. trade surplus with Mexico *should reach* $9 billion by 1995. . ."

> Here are three common ways of predicting future effects:
>
> a. will ultimately (create/cause/lead to/result in/grow to) . . .
>
> b. we're going to see ...
>
> c. should* (cause/reach/lead to/result in). . .
>
> * "Should" here has a different meaning from the more typical meaning of recommending an action.

Make predictions based on the following situations. Introduce each prediction with expression a, b, or c as indicated.

Example: Predict the effect of the treaty on the creation of jobs in the U.S.(b)

We're going to see a net gain of 130,000 U.S. jobs by 1995.

1. Make a prediction about the your country's economic growth in the next five years. (a)

   _____

2. Make a prediction about the effects of new regional trade blocks on your country's industries. (c)

   _____

3. Make a prediction about your government's future actions regarding trade issues.(b)

   _____

4. Make a prediction about the effects of new technologies on business in the future. (a)

   _____

5. Make a prediction about one particular company's competitiveness in 10 years. (b)

VOCABULARY CHECK

The words in *italics* are used in the video. Cross out the word in each row that does not have a similar meaning to the word in *italics*.

1. *hammer out*	set	destroy	come to agreement on
2. *motivation*	desire	reason	opportunity
3. *fringe benefits*	perks	extras	taxes
4. *retrain*	put aside	teach again	help learn new skills
5. *dislocated*	disrupted	promoted	put out of place or job

6. *model*	excuse	example	ideal
7. *opposition*	support	resistance	disagreement
8. *penalty*	loss	reward	disadvantage

DISCUSSION

Work in groups. Discuss your answers to the following questions.

1. How are (or would) your country's industries (be) affected by free trade? Be as specific as you can in discussing such industries as agriculture, automobiles and auto parts, computers and communications, clothing and textiles, electronics, etc.

2. What do you think business leaders in your country should do to remain competitive in your country's market? In other markets overseas?

3. What do you think your country's government leaders should do, if anything, to protect local business interests against foreign competition?

4. How would your country's industries be affected by regional trade blocks, such as
   a. the European Community's 1992 agreement
   b. the North American Free Trade Agreement

ROLE PLAY

Work in pairs. One student will play the role of a foreign business executive. The other student will play the role of a government official. Read the situation and the role descriptions below and decide who will play each role. After a ten-minute preparation, begin the negotiation.

THE SITUATION: **Trade Access Negotiation**

A foreign cellular phone manufacturer has been facing much resistance from the government trade office of _____ (your choice of country) in getting access to the that country's market. A meeting has been arranged for the two parties to hammer out some kind of agreement. [If you want to change the type of manufacturer, you may do so.]

ROLE DESCRIPTION: **Foreign Business Executive**

Your company has been trying to gain access to the market of _____ (name of country) to sell high quality, world-class cellular phones but has been repeatedly rejected by that country's government. At last, you have been granted a meeting with a government trade official. Prepare a list of exactly what you want to sell, how this product will help the country, how many units you want to sell, where in the country you want to sell them, and what you will do with the sales profits. Be prepared to answer government official's questions. Negotiate the best possible deal.

ROLE DESCRIPTION: **Government Trade Official**

You want to increase trade opportunities for your country's businesses and to protect those businesses from foreign competition, but you have been pressured from inside and outside your country to open up opportunities for foreign businesses. A meeting with a foreign executive has been arranged to work out an agreement about selling cellular phones in your country. Prepare a list of questions about what the executive's company wants to sell, why, where, and how. Try to get the executive to commit to investing all profits inside your country, possibly forming a partnership with a local company and/or setting up a manufacturing plant in your country. Negotiate the best possible deal.

READING

Read the following excerpts from Matthew Lynn's article, "Free at Last?," about the 1992 single market project of the European Community (EC). Then answer the questions that follow.

FREE AT LAST?

An open city or a fortress? If one question has imperilled the single market project it is this. To Europeans 1992 has appeared as a symbol of openness and of market liberalization. Outside Europe, particularly in the US and Japan, it has just as often appeared as a closed market.

There is a tension at the heart of the 1992 program that revolves around its objectives. In one sense it is an exercise in free trade aimed at breaking down barriers to commerce. But its proposers

also have in their sights the revitalization of European industry to compete with the challenge from Japan and the US.

The two objectives can be reconciled only by a formula refined with staggering success by the Japanese: internal freedom coupled with external protection. Thus, despite repeated protestations of innocence by the European Community, the myth of Fortress Europe has persisted in the outside world. From that perspective it seems the only logical way for the Community to achieve its goals. . . .

The Community's actions have provided much ammunition for those who accuse the Twelve* of covert protectionism. Three devices in particular have provoked the suspicions of Europe's trading partners: anti-dumping action, reciprocal deals and informal quotas.

Under General Agreement on Tariffs and Trade (GATT) rules, if the Commission can establish that foreign goods are being dumped — priced at less than in their home markets or for less than a 'reasonable' profit — then retaliation can be taken against the offenders. . . . Not only do anti-dumping actions introduce protectionism under cover of GATT rules, they are also flexible. The 'reasonable profit' clause allows the Commission to hit almost anyone who is causng domestic manufacturers pain. It has not spurned the opportunity. . . . Most actions conern will-organized industries such as electronics where pressure from industry groups for protection is heaviest. . . .

On a wider scale it has been willing to court the disapproval of the world trading regime by embracing reciprocal deals. It is an article of faith in world commerce that trading regions should not do special deals with one another. The system is supposed to work through GATT, with all participants having equal access to one another's markets on the same terms. However, the EC has shown a tendency to sidestep GATT in favor of reciprocal deals that allow foreign companies access to Europe to the same extent that European companies have access to the foreigners' markets. . . .

The third, and most blatant piece in the EC's protectionist armor has been the use of informal quotas. The Community is divided between members that have basically open markets, such as the UK and Germany, and others, such as Italy and France, that have strict quotas in particular industries on non-EC imports.

Nowhere is this more apparent than in the motor industry. France and Italy to a big extent, and other countries to a lesser extent, have kept out Japanese imports (which are invariably popular where drivers have the choice). This poses a problem for the Community. The completion of the internal market not only makes quotas wrong in theory, it makes them impractical. With the removal of border controls, there will be little to stop cars moving from Ireland, which has a completely free market, to France, which does not.

Germany's Mercedes-Benz has attacked any calls to replace national quotas with other forms of protection. But French and Italian carmakers have been pushing for European quotas to be imposed on the Japanese. The demand is made more complicated by the Japanese car plants in the UK. Late last year the Commission struck a 'gentleman's agreement' with the Japanese motor manufacturers under which Japan will monitor exports to the EC and ensure they do not exceed 1.2 million cars a year by 1999. The total EC market by then is expected to be 15.1 million cars. If such a deal is struck bilaterally and limiting imports, is not protectionist, then what is? . . .

The outcome is hardly a victory for free trade, but it does show how strong the pressures for protection can be, particularly in a major industry. And it illustrates the Commission's inability to resist such pressures, even though it knows it should. Its heart may be in the right place, but its actions are not. . . .

*The Twelve—The 12 nations that are members of the European Community.

Adapted and reprinted with permission of *International Magazine*; excerpts from "Free at Last?" by Matthew Lyon, January 1992, pp. 29–31.

1. How does the European Community's single market project appear to Europeans? How does it appear to people outside Europe?

   _____

   _____

   _____

2. What are the two objectives of the 1992 program?

   a. _____

   b. _____

   _____

3. What trade formula, successfully refined by the Japanese, does the EC seem to be following?

   _____

   _____

4. What are the three devices the EC has used to protect its industries? Briefly explain each device.

   a. _____   _____

   _____

   b. _____   _____

   _____

   c. _____   _____

   _____

5. What is the author's opinion of the EC's actions? _____

   _____

WRITING

Complete one of the following activities.

1. You work for a company that has been or will be affected negatively by free trade in your own market or by protectionism in foreign markets. Write a brief 200-250 word report, stating the problem, analyzing the situation, and recommending action to your CEO.

2. You are a consumer who is very unhappy about your inability to buy certain foreign goods because of government quotas or heavy tariffs on those goods. Write a letter of 200-250 words to the proper government official or agency.

Segment 7
Corporate Quality in the U.S.

From: Business World, 11/15/87
Begin: 35:16
Length: 6:12
Note: This segment is not closed captioned.

BEFORE YOU WATCH

TALKING POINTS

Work in groups. Discuss your answers to the following questions.

1. What exactly does the word 'quality' mean to you when you think of the following items:
   a. an automobile
   b. a home stereo
   c. clothes
   d. food
   e. a restaurant
   f. _____ (your choice)
2. List some examples of specific product brand names that you think of as having high quality, e.g., Rolex watches.
3. Have consumers changed their thinking about quality in the last 20 years? If so, how? If not, explain why not.

PREDICTING

The video is about the pursuit of quality in American industry in the 1980's. Write down your answers to the following questions. Then compare your answers with those of another student.

1. What do you already know about the pursuit of quality in American industry in the 1980's?

_____

_____

2. What are you unsure of about the topic?

_____

_____

3. What do you expect to learn from the video?

_____

_____

KEY WORDS

The *italicized* words in the sentences below will help you understand the video. Study the sentences. Then match the words with the meanings.

1. The *expectations* people have of cars like Mercedes are very high.

2. There is a *significant gap* between the quality of a Mercedes and a Yugo.

3. Everyone wants to buy goods that are high in quality; nobody wants to buy *shoddy* goods.

4. A *defective* product doesn't work the way it is supposed to.

5. The company has a solid *reputation* for high-quality products and good service.

6. We don't build in *obsolescence* into our products. The longer our products last, the more of them we sell.

7. The *warranty* on the car is for 3 years or 36,000 miles bumper-to-bumper. I can buy an extended warranty for 7 years at the time of purchase.

8. Many executives say that the *payoff* from quality control is very quick. Once customers see quality, they start buying.

1. _____ *expectation*   a. opinion which people generally have about someone or something

2. _____ *significant gap* b. written guarantee for a product

3. _____ *shoddy*   c. large difference

4. _____ *defective*   d. benefit (It also has a different, bad meaning)

5. _____ *reputation*   e. hope or belief

6. _____ *obsolescence*   f. process or condition of being old and not useful

7. _____ *warranty*   g. inferior, low-quality

8. _____ *payoff*   h. flawed, imperfect, containing errors

35:38–
41:18

GETTING THE MAIN IDEA

Watch the news report and listen for the answers to the following questions. Take brief notes on the answers. Then compare your answers with those of another student.

What happened to some American companies in the 80's? **Why?**

How has Corning Glass made improvements in quality?

How has Eastman Kodak made improvements

What are some of the business problems related to quality?

What?	
Why?	
How/Corning Glass?	
How/Eastman Kodak?	
What/problems?	

35:38–
36:01

WHAT'S MISSING

Listen again to Sander Vanocur's introduction to the news report. Fill in the missing words.

Sander Vanocur: The merchandise trade (1) _____ mean Americans are consuming more (2) _____ -made goods while the rest of the world consumes fewer American-made goods. What happened to the days when (3) _____ a new car meant choosing between a Chevy and a Ford, not a Toyota or Nissan? When

(4) _____ meant RCA or Zenith, not Sony or Panasonic? Business editor Stephen Aug reports it may take a look back to force a (5) _____ ahead.

IDENTIFYING WHAT YOU SEE

Watch the next part of the video with the sound off. Match the time codes with the things you see on the video.

1. 36:06-36:08 ___
2. 36:09-36:16 ___
3. 36:17-36:21 ___
4. 36:27-36:31 ___
5. 36:32-36:36 ___
6. 36:37-36:43 ___

a. a woman on a ladder dropping a radio
b. auto workers making cars a long time ago
c. a TV commercial for a washing machine
d. a TV commercial for a watch
e. a modern automobile assembly plant
f. a car driving over a bridge

CHECKING WHAT YOU HEAR

Watch the commercials on the video an check (✔) the products that are mentioned.

1. ☐ '87 Chevrolet trucks
2. ☐ '57 Chevrolet trucks
3. ☐ an automobile made in the USA
4. ☐ a JVC portable radio
5. ☐ a Westinghouse product
6. ☐ a Seiko watch

NOTETAKING

Watch the next part of the video and take brief notes on the answers to the following questions. Then compare your notes with those of another student.

1. What was the number one example used in the attack on American quality in 1987?

_____

2. What did Robert Stempel think about quality and expectations?

_____

3. What was Stempel's view of his own company's products in 1987?

_____

4. What did Dan Howell think about Stempel's company's products?

_____

INFORMATION MATCH

Watch the next part of the video. Match the companies with the correct information.

37:36–39:52

     a. Xerox   b. Corning Glass   c. Eastman Kodak   d. Levi-Strauss

1. _____ "We had the business, and all of a sudden, the Japanese came in and were eating our lunch."
2. _____ Has never lost its reputation for producing quality goods.
3. _____ Reduced defects in one area from 32% to under 2% in four years.
4. _____ Put in a total quality system, made the best quality in the world, and is shipping products to Japan.
5. _____ Was the pioneer and continues to lead.
6. _____ Has improved quality by expanding worker responsibility.
7. _____ Doesn't build obsolescence into its products.
8. _____ Its leader says that U.S. business lost track of where it was going for awhile and focused only on the domestic market.

LISTENING FOR DETAILS

Watch the last part of the video. Check the correct answers.

39:53–41:08

1. What happens when you say "quality" to someone from Wall Street?
   a. They become excited.
   b. They begin asking many specific questions.
   c. They become bored.
2. What does senior management too often reward?
   a. What happens in the short term.
   b. What happens in mergers and acquisitions.
   c. What happens in the long term.
3. What was one problem David Nadler found in a plant which has strict quality standards?
   a. They enforced the standards for three months and went on strike.
   b. They relaxed the standards because of the need to meet quotas.
   c. They stopped being concerned about quality after winning a national "Quality" award.
4. Compared to U.S. firms, what was the cost of turning out shoddy products at Japanese companies in the 80's?
   a. Lower.
   b. Higher.
   c. The same.
5. What is involved in driving up the cost of producing shoddy products?
   a. Warranty costs, repair costs, returned goods.
   b. Scrap costs & customer complaint departments.
   c. Both a & b.

CHECKING YOUR PREDICTIONS

Look at your answers to the PREDICTING exercise on pages 61 and 62. What did you learn about quality in the U.S. in the 1980's from the video? Was it what you expected to learn? (You may want to watch the video again.)

AFTER YOU WATCH

LANGUAGE POINT: CONDITIONAL SENTENCES

On the video, David Nadler uses an untrue conditional when he says, "If the customers were satisfied, they wouldn't call up and need help." What he means is that customers are calling up and needing help, so they are unsatisfied. (Untrue conditionals use the simple past tense in the "if" clause, and would + simple form in the result clause. True conditionals, on the other hand, use the simple present tense in the "if" clause, and will + simple form in the result clause, e.g., "If the customers are satisfied, they won't call up.") Change the sentences below from true to untrue or from untrue to true. The first one has been done for you.

1. (Untrue condition) If the customers *were* satisfied, they *wouldn't* call
   up and need help.
   (True condition) <u>If the customers **are** satisfied, they **won't** call up and
   need help.</u>

2. (True condition) If you <u>turn out</u> shoddy products, the customers <u>will</u>
   disappear.
   (Untrue condition) _____

3. (Untrue condition) If you <u>thought</u> only about the domestic market,
   your competitors <u>would go</u> right by you.
   (True condition) _____

4. (True condition) If we <u>maintain</u> a total quality management system, we
   <u>will become</u> the best in the world.
   (Untrue condition) _____

5. (Untrue condition) If the company <u>made</u> the improvements, it <u>would</u>
   <u>still be</u> in business.
   (True condition) _____

VOCABULARY CHECK: IDIOMS

The following sentences are from the video. What do the idioms in *italics* mean? Circle the answer that is closest in meaning.

1. . . . it may take a *look back* to force a step ahead.
   a. remember the past
   b. watch what is behind us
   c. distract ourselves

2. David Kearns says, "It's not so much a matter that the United States slipped; it's that we *lost track of* what was going on around the rest of the world . . .
   a. couldn't compete with
   b. no longer knew
   c. didn't care about

3. . . . particularly out in the Pacific Rim because they *went right by* us, as far as the issue of reliability and quality.
   a. worked in different directions than
   b. equalled and then got better than
   c. were taught by

4. We had the business, and all of a sudden the Japanese came in and were *eating our lunch*, they were taking it away from us.
   a. making deals with us
   b. spying on our research efforts
   c. taking our business customers

5. Yet quality often *takes a back seat* to a quick fix on the bottom line because of pressure from Wall Street.
   a. gets overlooked in favor of
   b. is handled better by
   c. is developed together with

6. . . . when you say "quality" to somebody from Wall Street their eyes *glaze over*.
   a. look bored
   b. look interested
   c. perk up in excitement

7. . . . the cost of *turning out* shoddy goods runs about 3% of revenues . . .
   a. rejecting
   b. producing
   c. selling

8. . . . you turn out shoddy goods, that customer is going to go elsewhere . . . And that's one customer who could be *gone for good*.
   a. is leaving for a better product.
   b. is always looking for quality
   c. is leaving and will not return.

DISCUSSION

Work in groups. Discuss your answers to the following questions.

1. What do you know about quality circles, total quality management (TQM) and other well-known quality approaches and techniques? If you don't know anything about them, what do you think they might be? If you know one approach, discuss its pros and cons. If you know two or more, compare them and discuss their pros and cons.

2. Choose one or two companies that you know . What has been done and is being done to improve the quality or their goods or services? What do you think of their progress so far? What more do they need to do to be able to compete successfully in the future?

ROLE-PLAY

Work in pairs. One student will play the role of a salesperson. The other student will play the role of a customer who is very concerned about the quality of the product or service and other related issues. Design your own role-play by choosing a product you know quite well. After choosing the product and taking ten minutes to prepare, begin your role-play.

THE SITUATION: **A Sales Representative-Customer Interaction**

A sales representative is discussing the merits of a product, of the pair's choice, with a potential customer. The customer needs to have a lot of information before making a decision.

ROLE DESCRIPTION: **Customer**

You are very interested in this product, but you are concerned with its quality and a number of related issues, for example, safety, reputation for excellence, reliability, warranty, repair record, customer complaints, service, style, choice of features, etc. Prepare a detailed list of questions for the sales representative about the information you need to know.

ROLE DESCRIPTION: **Sales Representative**

You are the sales representative for this product. Be prepared to answer a variety of questions about quality, and related issues, for example, reputation for excellence, reliability, warranty, repair record, customer complaints, service, style, choice of features, etc. Also prepare to make your communication as smooth and persuasive as you possibly can.

READING

Read the following excerpts from Brad Kuhn's article, "Companies in Search of Quality," in the Orlando Sentinel newspaper. Then answer the questions that follow.

COMPANIES IN SEARCH OF QUALITY

Leaders look for ways to improve the delivery of goods and services

Jim Rose can't stand mistakes. The 32-year-old master electrician . . . makes wiring harnesses for ambulances, and he knows that a defect could be disastrous. "We're not just building recreational vehicles, we're building something that's going to save your life," he said. "If we have something that's not correct, it can cost a life."

Quality in workmanship or service isn't always a matter of life or death, but it is a big deal for businesses — accounting for $1 of every $4 in sales. With poor quality control, most of that money is spent on fixing mistakes; with zero defects, it goes to the bottom line.

Simply defined, quality is giving customers what they want, when they want it, consistently.

. . . The real quality battles are being fought on the shop floors and in the boardrooms of businesses... They all have their gurus...the most popular are Joseph M. Juran and W. Edwards Deming, two consultants who gained international fame for teaching quality control to the Japanese after World War II. Japan's highest honor for quality management in named for Deming.

But many companies have found that the theories of quality are not easily applied. In the 1970's the popular thinking was that the Japanese success came from superior technology—robots. General Motors invested heavily in automating its production lines, causing an uproar among employees who feared they would be replaced by machines. The automaker and others quickly discovered that robots were not simply mechanical employees. They were highly specialized tools that could speed up repetitive processes. But they could also lead to bottlenecks farther down the line. And while workers could be retrained, robots were limited by their own technology.

By the early 1980's, quality circles became all the rage as industry attempted to give workers more autonomy. The groups were envisioned as employee-run think tanks. But most failed, experts say, because they lacked management support. Without guidance, quality circles tended to gravitate toward cosmetic issues, such as parking or the quality of food in the company cafeteria.

Companies tried other quality-improvement approaches and began measuring anything that could be measured to find the cost of defects and the value of improvements. Florida Power & Light of Miami gained international recognition in 1989 as the first U.S. company to win the Deming award. The utility had hired Japanese management consultants and spent $1.5 million to set up ways to measure customer service. The result: FPL earned a 57 percent increase in reliability and a 65 percent decrease in on-the-job injuries. Customer complaints dropped to a 10-year low. But some employees complained that the new system buried them in paperwork. The company chairman agreed, and by the time the award was announced, FPL had scrapped many of the changes.

Later in the 1980's, key elements of quality, employee participation, leadership and measurement—began to come together under the umbrella of Total Quality Management. It was a giant leap from previous ideas, but companies have found there is still a big difference between theory and reality.

. . . Influenced by the the teachings of Deming and Juran, Harris Corporation's manager in 1983 concluded that 85% of its quality problems were beyond the control of employees, and they needed to be fixed by improving the system. That shift in mind-set created three new objectives:

• Departments should consider themselves each other's suppliers and customers. That is, work performed for another department should be held to the same standards as work performed for an outside customer.

• Managers should act more like coaches

and less like cops, encouraging innovation through recognition, training and advancement—rather than by threatening employees with penalties.

• The company should train employees in problem solving and analysis techniques and work to resolve a problem jointly. . . .

Adapted and reprinted with permission of *The Orlando Sentinel*, Central Florida Business Section, excerpts of "Companies in Search of Quality", by Brad Kuhn, August 17–23, 1992, pp. 14–15.

1. What definition of quality is given? _____
2. What have many companies found about applying theories of quality? _____
   _____
3. What did General Motors do in the 1970's? _____
4. Was it as successful as planned? _____
5. What became popular in the early 1980's? _____
6. What happened to it? _____
   _____
7. Why? _____
8. What did Florida Power & Light of Miami do? _____
9. Was it successful? _____
10. What problems were caused by the changes? _____
11. What did the company then decide to do? _____
12. What three things are part of Total Quality Management, according to the author? _____
    _____
13. What were the three objectives set by Harris Corp. in 1983?
    a. _____
    b. _____
    c. _____

WRITING

Complete one of the following activities.

1. You work for a company that needs to make quality improvements in some specific areas. Write a one-page report, stating one problem area, the reasons that change is needed, your recommendation for change, and the reasons for that particular recommendation.
2. Pick a product you know and analyze it for quality and features. Write a letter to the Director of Marketing, suggesting ways that the company could improve the product's quality, expand on its features, or improve service or some other aspect of the product.

Segment 8
Chrysler/Ford Profits

From: Business World, 8/2/92
Begin: 41:31
Length: 4:83
Note: This segment is not closed captioned.

BEFORE YOU WATCH

TALKING POINTS

Work in groups. Discuss your answers to the following questions.

1. When buying a car, what things are most important to you, e.g., price, reputation of the car or company, basic quality, engine power, design, comfort, fuel efficiency, safety features, warranty, repair record, dealer service, special features, salesperson's attitude & behavior, etc.?

2. What do you know about the recent history, i.e., the last 15 years, of Ford, Chrysler, and General Motors? How are they similar? How are they different? Are there companies in your country with similar histories?

3. How do recessions, or bad economic times, affect the auto industry in your country? How do recessions affect other industries, e.g., agriculture, banking, construction, electronics, etc.?

PREDICTING

Based on the title of the video segment, what do you think you will see and hear on the video? Write down five items under each of the headings below. Then compare your answers with those of another student.

	SIGHTS (things you expect to see)	**WORDS** (words you expect to hear)
1.	_____	_____
2.	_____	_____
3.	_____	_____
4.	_____	_____
5.	_____	_____

KEY WORDS

The *italicized* words in the sentences below will help you understand the video. Study the sentences. Then write your own definition of each word.

1. After years of *red ink* and tough times, the company finally earned a profit and is now in the black.

   red ink: _____

2. *Profit margins* in some types of retail stores are about 10%, but in supermarkets, profits are lower; margins are usually only about 1-2%.

   profit margins: _____

3. There are very wide *disparities* between the salaries of top executives and the wages of the workers, especially in the U.S.

   disparities: _____

4. Two cars may be *comparably equipped*, with similar quality and features, but one might sell for more money for various reasons.

   comparably equipped: _____

5. Japanese *market share* has increased a lot in auto markets all over the world in the last 20 years.

   market share: _____

6. *Consumer confidence* generally falls is bad economic times and rises in good economic times.

   consumer confidence: _____

7. The company's earnings this last year were *modest*, much lower than the top executives had hoped for.

   modest: _____

8. The economy in the U.S. was in a *recession* from 1990 through1992; other nations have been experiencing similarly bad economic times.

   recession: _____

GETTING THE MAIN IDEA

Watch the news report and listen for the answers to the following questions. Take brief notes on the answers. Then compare your answers with those of another student.

41:47–
46:06

> **Who** is doing **what**?
>
> **Why** is this happening?
>
> **How** are the Japanese car makers at a disadvantage?

CHECKING YOUR PREDICTIONS

Look at the lists you made in the PREDICTING exercise on page 72. Watch the video again and check (✔) the items that you actually see and hear.

41:47–
46:06

Who?	
What?	
Why?	
How?	

WHAT'S MISSING?

Listen again to Stephen Aug's introduction to the news report. Fill in the missing words.

41:47–
42:06

Stephen Aug: After months of driving through (1) _____ ink, two U.S. auto makers have found the (2) _____ at the end of the tunnel. Ford posted a second quarter (3) _____ of $502 million. More surprisingly, Chrysler showed a second quarter profit of (4) $_____ million. Those figures raised the question: even if Detroit is leading, will the rest of the (5) _____ follow?

42:06–
42:51

WHO'S WHO

Look at the chart below. Then watch the next part of the video and check
(✔) the appropriate boxes. You may need to watch the video several times
to complete the exercise.

Who . . .?	Michael Towers	Farrell Furst	Jeff Monninger
1. thinks the new Jeep has a unique design			
2. thinks the Jeep rides great & is comfortable			
3. likes the fact that the Jeep is American			
4. is very pleased with large volume of sales			
5. is surprised by how popular the Jeep is			
6. thinks the Jeep has everything you want			

42:51–
44:00

MAKING TRUE SENTENCES

Watch the next part of the video. Then use the chart below to make six true
sentences. Write the sentences. You may need to watch the video several
times to complete the exercise. The first one has been done for you.

Stephen Aug reports that . . .	1. . . . Chrysler's line of lightweight trucks has been a strong profit center.
Mary Ann Keller states that . . .	2. . . . there are wide disparities in price between Japanese & U.S. vehicles.
Albert Vitarelli says that . . .	3. . . . Chrysler earns about $5,000 in profit per minivan.
Joseph Phillippi notes that . . .	4. . . . it's the Big Three again and they're coming out with good stuff.
	5. . . . a comparably equipped Saturn is $3,000 less than a Honda Accord.
	6. . . . profit margins on trucks sales are almost double those on car sales.

1. *Stephen Aug reports that Chrysler's line of lightweight trucks has been a strong profit center.*

2. _____

3. _____

4. _____

5. _____

6. _____

NOTETAKING

Watch the rest of the video and take brief notes on the answers to the following questions. Then compare your notes with those of another student.

44:01–
45:56

1. How was consumer confidence at this time?

   _____

2. Why was there a build-up of need for vehicles at this time?

   _____

3. How will these trends benefit General Motors?

   _____

4. How has the popularity of Ford and Chrysler cars and trucks affected General Motors?

   _____

5. What does the Ford treasurer feel about the economy?

   _____

LANGUAGE POINT: SHOWING DIFFERENCE OR CONTRAST

On the video, Stephen Aug contrasts the situation between American and Japanese auto makers by saying, "*Unlike* American car makers, the Japanese have been forced to raise prices.

Here are two common ways of showing difference or contrast:
a. Unlike . . .   b. In contrast to . . .

Show contrasts based on the following situations. Introduce each contrast with expression a or b as indicated.

Example: Show contrast between American car makers (who did not have to raise prices) and Japanese car makers (who had to raise prices). (b)

> *In contrast to American car makers, the Japanese had to raise prices.*

1. Show contrast between the improved situation of Ford and the situation at General Motors, which continues to struggle. (a)

   _____

2. Show contrast between the high increases in car sales following previous recessions and car sales in 1992. (b)

   _____

3. Show contrast between previous quarters (where Chrysler reported losses) and the second quarter of 1992 (where it showed a profit of $178 million). (a)

   _____

   _____

4. Show contrast between the large profit margins on truck sales and profit margins on car sales, which are only about half as much. (b)

   _____

   _____

5. Show contrast between a Honda Accord, priced at $14,560, and a comparably equipped Saturn, priced at $11,620. (b)

   _____

   _____

VOCABULARY CHECK

The words and phrases below are used on the video. Put each word or phrase into the appropriate category on the chart.

recession	come out with	recovery
profit margin	depression	launch
borrowing costs	market share	take off

ECONOMIC TERMS	COMPANY TERMS	COMPANY ACTIONS
_____	_____	_____
_____	_____	_____
_____	_____	_____

DISCUSSION

Work in groups. Discuss your answers to the following questions.

1. Ford and Chrysler have had aggressive quality improvement programs in the last decade and that's undoubtedly one of the reasons for their recent successes. However, a company's success depends on many factors, some of which were noted in the video. List and discuss all factors, both inside and outside the company that have impact on a company's success.

2. Choose one or two companies that you know well. Discuss how their business has been in the past, is at present, and probably will be in the next few years. What challenges must they face at the present and in the future?

3. How is the economy in your country doing at present? How has it done in the recent past? What are the prospects for economic growth in the future?

ROLE-PLAY

Work in threes. One student will play the role of meeting leader and analyst. The other students will play the roles of business analysts. Read the situation, the analysis grid, and the role descriptions and decide who will play each role. After a ten-minute preparation, begin the meeting.

THE SITUATION: **A Business Analysis Meeting**

Your consulting firm analyzes specific business companies and their competitors. Today, you are meeting with other consultants in your firm to analyze and discuss the strengths and weaknesses of companies in specific industries. Choose the industry you will analyze, e.g., automobiles, and the specific companies you will focus on, e.g., Toyota, Honda, Nissan, Mazda, BMW, Mercedes, Volvo, Peugeot, etc. Use the brief analysis grid below as a basic form. You may adapt and lengthen it if you so wish.

ANALYSIS GRID: **Strengths and Weaknesses**

	Performance					Importance	
	++	+	0	-	--	Hi	Lo
Marketing Strengths (reputation for quality & service, strong market share, low manufacturing & distribution costs, effective sales force, effective R & D, geographical advantage, etc.)	—	—	—	—	—	—	—
Financial Strengths (cost, availability, profitablity)	—	—	—	—	—	—	—
Manufacturing Strengths (well-equipped facilities, good capacity, solid work force, able to deliver on time, technical and manufacturing skill)	—	—	—	—	—	—	—
Organizational Strengths (visionary leadership, capable managers, dedicated workers, flexible and adaptable, speedy response to changing conditions)	—	—	—	—	—	—	—

(adapted and shortened from Philip Kotler, Marketing Management, Sixth Edition, Prentice Hall, Chapter 2, page 53)

ROLE DESCRIPTION: **Meeting Leader/Analyst**

You are the head consultant on this project. After your team decides which industry and companies to focus on, lead the discussion on the strengths and weaknesses of each company. As you do this, be sure to ask specific questions of the other consultants. After analyzing each company, your team should compare the companies and evaluate them overall for strengths and weaknesses. Prepare a list of questions and your own strategy for leading the meeting.

ROLE DESCRIPTION: **Consultant/Analyst for the Leading Companies**

You are the chief consultant on the two leading companies in the industry. As such, you need to give very thorough and specific information on the strengths and weaknesses of these companies. In this meeting, you will need to compare your information with that of another analyst. Prepare your own analysis before the meeting and be prepared to answer questions about your companies and to ask questions about other companies being analyzed.

ROLE DESCRIPTION: **Consultant/Analyst for Other Companies**

You are the chief consultant on the other companies in the industry. As such, you need to give very thorough and specific information on the strengths and weaknesses of these companies. In this meeting, you will need to compare your information with that of another analyst. Prepare your own analysis before the meeting and be prepared to answer questions about your companies and to ask questions about other companies being analyzed.

READING

Read the following article from *Business Week* and then fill out the grid that follows. Some of the information you need is given in the article and some must be inferred.

DETROIT'S NEW LEADERS AND THE TASKS THEY FACE

Chrysler has named a CEO-designate, GM has a new top operations man, and two prospects have emerged to succeed Ford's chief when he retires next year.

GENERAL MOTORS	FORD	CHRYSLER
President Jack Smith	Executive Vice-Presidents Alex Trotman and Allan Gilmour	Vice-Chairman Robert Eaton
STRENGTHS	**STRENGTHS**	**STRENGTHS**
• Strong European operations • Nonauto operations such as EDS and Hughes give profit cushion • Strong brands enhanced by new models, and more are coming	• Efficient manufacturing makes it a low-cost producer • Hit models such as Taurus and Explorer • Leading in new marketing techniques such as no-haggle pricing	• Booming minivan and Jeep sales • Classy new models on the way such as LH sedans, a subcompact, and a pickup • Has Detroit's leanest management structure
CHALLENGES	**CHALLENGES**	**CHALLENGES**
• Cut sky-high costs • Keep up employee morale during reorganization and retrenchment • Pare some models	• Speed up replacement of aging models • Turn around its money-losing Jaguar subsidiary • Catch up in engines and transmissions	• Shore up weak finances • Avoid snafus in new-model introductions • Drop either Eagle or Plymouth line to refocus brands

Reprinted from June 29, 1992 issue of *Business Week* by special permission, 1992 by McGraw-Hill, Inc., p. 84.

	General Motors	Ford	Chrysler

Product cost Ranking (best =1, next = 2, worst = 3)

	General Motors	Ford	Chrysler
Management structure Ranking (1,2,3)	_____	_____	_____
Finance situation ranking (1,2,3)	_____	_____	_____
Best in minivan market segment	_____	_____	_____
Tops in new marketing techniques	_____	_____	_____
Strongest in Europe	_____	_____	_____
Profits in nonauto operations	_____	_____	_____
Weak in engines	_____	_____	_____
Delays in introducing new models	_____	_____	_____
Too many models	_____	_____	_____

WRITING

Complete one of the following activities.

1. Write up a 250-300 word strengths and weaknesses analysis of the companies your group discussed in the role-play. Make it concise, yet thorough.

2. Write up an 250-300 comparative analysis of General Motors, Ford, and Chrysler, using the information grid you filled out for the reading as a general guide.

Segment 9

On the Road Again

From: 20/20, 1/25/91
Begin: 46:17
Length: 12:40

BEFORE YOU WATCH

TALKING POINTS

Work in groups. Discuss your answers to the following questions.

1. What are the pros and cons of travelling by motorcycle?

2. What kinds of people buy and ride motorcycles?

3. What images come to your mind when you think of very large motorcycles?

4. What images come to your mind, if any, when you think of Harley-Davidson?

PREDICTING

Work in groups. Based on the title of the news report, write down three questions you think will be answered on the video.

1. _____

2. _____

3. _____

KEY WORDS

The *italicized* words will help you understand the video. Study the definitions. Then use each word or phrase in a sentence of your own.

1. *establishment:* the powerful organizations and people in society.

_____

2. *loyalty:* faithfulness to someone or something.

_____

3. *mystique:* a feeling of mystery that surrounds certain people or things.

_____

4. *classic:* recognized as being of high quality and lasting value.

_____

5. *implicit:* expressed indirectly; only hinted at or suggested.

_____

6. *comeback:* a return to popularity or competitiveness after a bad time.

_____

7. *desperate gamble:* an extremely risky action.

_____

8. *financial outlook:* the future prospects of one's money situation.

_____

WHILE YOU WATCH

46:39–
58:50

GETTING THE MAIN IDEA

Watch the news report and listen for the answers to the following questions. Take brief notes on the answers. Then compare your answers with those of another student.

Who changed the motorcycling image of the 70's?

What did the manufacturers of Harley-Davidson **do** to profit from the 70's 'cycle boom?

What effect did this have on quality and sales?

When did Harley-Davidson motorcycles begin to make a comeback?

How did Harley **manage** to become successful again?

Who?	
What/do?	
What effect?	
When?	
How/manage?	

CHECKING YOUR PREDICTIONS

46:39–
58:50

Look at the questions you wrote in the PREDICTING exercise on page 81. Watch the video again. Which of your questions are answered on the video? What answers are given?

WHAT'S MISSING?

47:12–
47:40

Listen again to Barbara Walters' introduction to the news report. Fill in the missing words.

Barbara Walters: Here's a (1) _____ for you. What travels in packs, breathes (2) _____ and not long ago was an endangered species? The (3) _____ , the Harley-Davidson motorcycle. To their (4) _____ , it's the king of the road, a (5) _____ for Americans built by Americans, but at the height of its (6) _____ , the Harley almost suffered a wipe-out at the hand of (7) _____ competitors. Not so fast, said Harley. Stone Phillips has the story of the meanest bike on the (8) _____ .

WHAT DO YOU SEE?

47:41–
49:08

Watch the next part of the video with the sound off. Circle the things you see on the video. The first one has been done for you.

1. crowded city street / (empty road in the countryside)
2. motorcycle gang / one person on a small motorcycle
3. sandy road by the beach / highway by the mountains
4. business executives riding motorcycles / non-business people
5. man with a tattoo on his arm / man with a painting
6. new motorcycle on display / old motorcycle on display

TRUE OR FALSE?

Watch the beginning of the video again. Are the following statements *true* or *false*? Write **T** (true) or **F** (false). Make the false statements true by changing one or two words.

1. _____ Marlon Brando's *The Wild One* introduced good boys on good bikes.

2. _____ Many wild angels and easy riders have criss-crossed American highways in search of the real America.

3. _____ The freedom of the road and Harley-Davidson are related ideas to some people.

4. _____ After 1954, Harley-Davidson was one of the top three motorcycles made in America.

5. _____ Harley-Davidson motorcycles have not had loyal customers in the past.

6. _____ Harley-Davidson is considered an American institution.

CHECKING WHAT YOU HEAR

Watch the next part of the video and check (✔) the words that are used to describe Harley-Davidson motorcycles of the past.

1. ☐ work of art
2. ☐ masterpiece
3. ☐ "hog"
4. ☐ major advance in the science of transportation
5. ☐ practical
6. ☐ designed for pleasure
7. ☐ loud
8. ☐ never breaking down
9. ☐ unreliable
10. ☐ classics

MAKING TRUE SENTENCES

Watch the next part of the video. Then use the chart below to make six true sentences. Write the sentences below.

Harley-Davidson...	1. . . . offered more power, higher quality at lower cost in the 70's.
Japanese competitors...	2. . . . became a classic case of being left in the dark by overseas competition.
Honda...	3. . . . came up with a very effective marketing campaign.
	4. . . . tried to cash in on the cycle boom by tripling production.
	5. . . . implied in an ad that people who ride Harley's aren't necessarily the kind of people you'd like to meet.
	6. . . . moved in for the kill when quality became a big issue.

1. _____

2. _____

3. _____

4. _____

5. _____

6. _____

PUTTING EVENTS IN ORDER

52:25–54:45

Read the sentences below and on the following page. Then watch the next part of the video and put the events in the correct order. Number them 1 to 8. The first event has been numbered for you. These events give the reasons for Harley's comeback success.

_____ Harley executives borrowed $80 million to buy back the company.

_____ The company got U.S. tariff protection against Japanese motorcycles.

_____ Harley-Davidson came within days of going out of business.

_____ The company created new designs, stayed close to customers, and introduced Japanese quality production techniques.

_1_ The company went through a lot of lay-offs.

_____ Harley executives and investors went through some tough years.

_____ The company began licensing the old name and appealing to upscale customers.

_____ The company got a last-minute reprieve from a finance company and a $20 million stock offering.

NOTETAKING

54:52–58:44

Watch the rest of the video and take brief notes on the answers to the following questions. Then compare your notes with those of another student.

1. What store does the Harley-Davidson dealership look like?

   _____

2. How much does the motorcycle cost and who will buy it?

   _____

3. What kind of people are in this motorcycle gang?

   _____

4. What kind of people have given the company a lot of free publicity?

_____

5. What was Harley's market share of big bikes in the U.S. in 1991?—1995?

_____

6. What's the catch, or problem, with that news about market share?

_____

7. What is Harley doing about this problem? Where?

_____

8. What is Harley's pitch "When you buy a Harley, you . . .?"

_____

9. What aces did Harley have up its sleeve?

_____

AFTER YOU WATCH

LANGUAGE POINT: SHOWING AND EMPHASIZING RELATIONSHIPS

On the video, Stone Phillips uses the expression, "not just . . . but" to emphasize a point about the Harley motorcycle when he says, "To its owners, Harley is *not just* transportation, *but* a work of patriotic American art." Change the sentences below so that they use "not just . . . but".

1. Japanese quality production techniques are valued in Japan. They are valued all the world as well.

_____

2. Harley-Davidson's story is an important one for American business. It is an important one for business organizations everywhere.

_____

3. A company that stays close to the customer will change designs more quickly. It can maintain its market share in tough times.

_____

4. The Honda motorcycle in the 70's attracted many first-time riders. It also attracted buyers who did not respond to Harley's tough image.

_____

_____

VOCABULARY CHECK: IDIOMS

The following excerpts are from the video. What do the idioms in *italics* mean? Match the idioms with the meanings that follow.

1. Harley customers *became hooked on* the Harley mystique . . .

2. The joke that was *running around* at that time was that sometimes you had to have two Harley-Davidsons, one for spare parts, in order to keep one on the road.

3. To *cash in on* a 70's cycle boom, they tripled production . . .

4. . . . and quality *went bust*.

5. . . . the competition *moved in for the kill*.

6. Honda *came on the scene* . . .

7. Honda . . . *came up with* a very, very effective marketing campaign . . .

8. . . . Harley's share had plunged to under 31 percent and many Harley workers *were out in the cold*.

9. Lenders were *getting cold feet*.

10. . . . this is a company that *had aces up its sleeve*.

1. *became hooked on*	a. prepared to destroy an opponent
2. *running around*	b. becoming nervous
3. *cash in on*	c. developed
4. *went bust*	d. became terrible
5. *moved in for the kill*	e. arrived
6. *came on the scene*	f. fell in love with
7. *came up with*	g. had hidden advantages
8. were *out in the cold*	h. take advantage of
9. getting *cold feet*	i. had lost their jobs
10. had *aces up its sleeve*	j. being told in different places

DISCUSSION

Work in groups. Discuss your answers to the following questions.

1. What did you learn from the video?

2. In the 70's, Harley-Davidson tripled production and quality went bust. What are the pros and cons of increasing production in good times?

3. Could Harley's turnaround and comeback be done by most other companies in trouble? Why or why not?

ROLE-PLAY

Work in threes. One student will play the role of the marketing manager. The other students will play the roles of marketing design specialists. Read the situation and the role descriptions below and decide what your customized situation will be and who will play each role. After a ten-minute preparation, begin the meeting.

THE SITUATION: **A Marketing Campaign Planning Meeting**

Your consulting company is preparing a marketing campaign for one of its clients. Choose *your situation* by selecting any one item from each column below, and design your campaign around it (i.e. automobile, 1 year on market, average reputation, change image, target middle-income). If the product is already on the market, you may choose a real brand, e.g. Harley-Davidson.

PRODUCT	TIME ON MARKET	REPUTATION	OBJECTIVE	TARGET MARKET
automobile	5 years	none (new)	refresh image	lower-income
stereo	1 year	high quality	broaden appeal	middle-income
clothing	0 (new)	average	narrow target	teenagers
shampoo	10 years	low quality	change image	professionals
hotel	20 years	good in small market	build awareness	"rich and famous"

ROLE DESCRIPTION: **Marketing Manager**

You are the manager in charge of the marketing campaign. Prepare the agenda (list of items to be discussed at the meeting). You need to consider the type of product, its time on the market, its reputation, the campaign's objective, the target market AND what your competitors are doing. Your task is to lead the meeting and get a successful campaign idea to submit to your boss.

ROLE DESCRIPTION: **Marketing Design Specialists**

You are marketing design specialists who have been assigned to work on this campaign. Your task is to analyze the product, the market, and the competition, and then to design a successful campaign. At the very least, you need to come up with a sentence or slogan to express the campaign idea (e.g., Honda's "You meet the nicest people on a Honda.") Prepare your list of ideas.

READING

Read the following excerpts from an article by James B. Shuman in Business Tokyo and then fill in the grid that follows.

EASY RIDER RIDES AGAIN

. . . Harley-Davidson, founded in 1903, is a piece of pure Americana. Its motorcycles are icons of independence, freedom, and adventure. In the 1980's, however, the company found itself riding against a recession, poor-quality products and relentless pressure from Japanese competitors. How the company fought back—by understanding its role in the American imagination and developing a unique relationship with its customers—offers valuable lessons for executives on both sides of the Pacific. . . .

Harley-Davidson's innovative program had five facets:

• Prove that the quality problems are over. Potential buyers had to be convinced that Harley was once again making quality motorcycles. The company spent $3 million on an unprecedented demonstrated program called SuperRide. A series of television commercials invited bikers to come to any of the company's more than 600 dealers for a ride on a new motorcycle. Over three weekends, more than 40,000 people showed up. SuperRide didn't sell enough bikes to cover its cost, but many who rode the demonstrators came back to buy a year or two later.

• Define the niche. In the 1970's, Harley had tried to compete against Japanese imports by marketing small Italian-made motorcycles. In the 1980's, it focused on what it knew best, American-made super-heavyweights.

• Listen to customers. Harley officials set out to talk with customers. "We didn't do focus groups or use one-way mirrors," says Jerry Wilke, vice-president for sales and marketing. "We got on a motorcycle and had fun with them." Harley executives turned up all over the United States on weekends. . . The gut feel was that customers wanted motorcycles that looked like the bikes of the 1940's but were reliable and technologically up-to-date.

• Use imaginative advertising. In the early days of the Harley-Davidson leveraged buyout, money was tight. Harley slashed its 1985 ad budget from $1.2 million to $180,000. The company made up for the cut with humorous advertisements that sold the Harley image, not speed or mechanical features. One showed a Malcolm Forbes balloon in the shape of a Harley floating over the heads of a crowd. "Thank God, they don't leak anymore," it said.

• Improve dealers. Harley also tackled the problems of dealers whose image was more Hell's Angels than wholesome family fun. The company raised standards, trained dealers and penalized those who didn't shape up. Many dealers balked at the moves and formed their own association in protest, but the company succeeded in bringing them back into the fold. . . .

Today Harley-Davidson is an unqualified success.

1. Three words used to describe the meaning of Harley:

   _____ _____ _____

2. Harley's decision on how to compete with Japanese competitors:

   _____

3. The five facets of Harley's marketing campaign:

   a. _____

   b. _____

   c. _____

   d. _____

   e. _____

WRITING

Complete one of the following activities.

1. As a marketing consultant, write an executive summary of 200-250 words of the marketing campaign you designed during the role play exercise above, detailing the most important points clearly and concisely.

2. As a marketing consultant, write an executive summary of 200-250 words, detailing how you would advise a competitor of Harley's to try to increase its market share.

Segment 10

Flexibility of Companies to Workers' Family Care Needs

Child Care

From: World News Tonight, 11/27/87
Begin: 59:00
Length: 5:16

BEFORE YOU WATCH

TALKING POINTS

Work in groups. Discuss your answers to the following questions.

1. What kinds of benefits do established businesses, including multinational companies, in your country offer to their workers?

2. How do these benefits for employees help the business, if at all?

3. What kinds of benefits would you, as a company employee, like to have a company provide for you?

4. Are the numbers of women in the workforce in your country changing? If so, how much? If not, why not?

5. How could increased numbers of women in the workforce lead to changes in companies and cultures?

PREDICTING

Based on the title of the video segment and the questions above, what do you think you will see and hear on the video? List five items under each of the headings on the following page. Then compare your answers with those of another student.

| SIGHTS | WORDS |
| (things you expect to see) | (words you expect to hear) |

1. _____   _____

2. _____   _____

3. _____   _____

4. _____   _____

5. _____   _____

KEY WORDS

The *italicized* words in the sentences below will help you understand the video. Study the sentences. Then match the words with the meanings.

1. After the end of World War II in 1945, there was a big *baby boom*, which led to more children in schools in the 50's and 60's.

2. Companies that want to remain competitive use *innovative* ideas.

3. Credit cards have caused a *revolution* in people's spending habits.

4. A company's business *philosophy* will guide its important decisions.

5. Every year, business organizations send representatives to universities to *recruit* new graduates into the companies.

6. If the secretary gets sick, the boss may decide to hire a *temporary* until the secretary returns.

7. One personnel problem that some fast food restaurants face is the rapid *turnover* of its workers.

8. The computer has helped many corporations to improve the *productivity* of their operations.

1. _____ *baby boom*   a. try to get new people to join

2. _____ *innovative*   b. short-term worker

3. _____ *revolution*   c. beliefs, attitudes, and values

4. _____ *philosophy*   d. very big and basic change

5. _____ *recruit*   e. new and original; progressive

6. _____ *temporary*   f. rate of getting results

7. _____ *turnover*   g. rise in the number of births

8. _____ *productivity*   h. numbers of people hired to replace those who stopped working

WHILE YOU WATCH

GETTING THE MAIN IDEA

Watch the news report and listen for the answers to the following questions. Take brief notes on the answers. Then compare your answers with those of another student.

59:14–
01:03:50

How are some American companies changing?

Why are they doing this?

Why are some other companies still **not** doing this?

How?	
Why?	
Why not?	

CHECKING YOUR PREDICTIONS

Look at the lists you made in the PREDICTING exercise on page 92. Watch the video and check (✔) the items that you actually see and hear.

59:14–
01:03:50

WHAT'S MISSING?

Listen again to Diane Sawyer's introduction to the news report. Fill in the missing words.

59:14–
59:38

Diane Sawyer: Tonight on the American Agenda, balancing work and (1) _____ . It used to be that American companies would tell their (2) _____ when you come to work leave your family (3) _____ at home. But that was before the homemakers started taking other (4) _____ . Now that the baby boom is over and skilled (5) _____ are in such demand, (6) _____ are entering the work force in record numbers. As Rebecca Chase tells us, that has forced some (7) _____ to change the way they do (8) _____ .

INFORMATION MATCH

Watch the video. Match the name of the company with the policy or benefit it offers its employees.

1. _____ Home Box Office (HBO)
2. _____ Stride Rite
3. _____ IBM
4. _____ Arthur Anderson
5. _____ Time Magazine

a. has an Elder Care Information and Referral Service

b. lets part-time employees become partners in the company

c. offers on-site day care for children and has a day-care center for elderly relatives

d. allows two part-time employees to share one job.

e. pays a trained worker to go to an employee's home when a child is sick

LISTENING FOR DETAILS

Watch the video. Circle the correct answers.

1. What is the quiet but dramatic revolution according to Rebecca Chase?
   a. Redefinition of jobs and the replacement of traditional career paths.
   b. Replacement of traditional career paths and restructuring of company benefits.
   c. Redefinition of jobs, replacement of traditional career paths and restructuring of company benefits.

2. What is the number one problem for employees?
   a. Keeping jobs in recessionary times.
   b. Getting new benefits and promotions.
   c. Having good child care.

3. How many companies provide some kind of help for this problem?
   a. 3,000.
   b. 4,000.
   c. 30,000.

4. How long has Stride Rite provided day-care for its employees?
   a. 20 years.
   b. 10 years.
   c. 2 months.

5. How does Arnold Hiatt of Stride Rite describe this investment?
   a. It improves earnings and provides return on the investment.
   b. It is the fair and caring thing to do for the employees.
   c. It helps the company to hire the best and the brightest.

6. What did IBM marketing manager, Jim Askew, do with the company's assistance?
   a. Find a day-care center for his two children.
   b. Find a retirement village near his home for his mother-in-law.
   c. Find a way to work part-time so that he could take care of his family needs.

7. Why does IBM do what it does, according to W.E. Burdick, IBM VP?
   a. Because employees want this.
   b. Because frustrated employees aren't going to focus on their work.
   c. Because employees are preoccupied with fringe benefits.

8. What does Carey Brown do?
   a. She is an advertising account manager.
   b. She is a marketing manager.
   c. She is an audit manager.

9. Which day of the week do Mary Jane Berrien and Susan Ostreich work together?
   a. Wednesday.
   b. Thursday.
   c. Friday.

10. Why does their work situation satisfy both them and their employer?
    a. They have more freedom and the company saves money.
    b. They spend more time with their children and the company's clients remain satisfied.
    c. They spend more time with their children and the company saves money.

NOTETAKING

Watch Rebecca Chase's conclusion to the news report and take brief notes on the answers to the following questions. Then compare your notes with those of another student.

01:03:08-
01:03:39

1. Do most employees enjoy the benefits mentioned in the news report? Why or why not?

_____

2. According to Rebecca Chase what will happen to companies that do not help employees balance work and family?

_____

LANGUAGE POINT: GIVING REASONS FOR ONE'S OPINIONS

On the video, Rebecca Chase notes what has been said and the reason for it when she reports that "Companies say the (benefits) are too expensive or not equitable **because** they cannot be used by everyone." The sentence could also be changed to "Because the benefits cannot be used by everyone, companies say they are too expensive or not equitable." Change sentences 1, 3, and 5 so that the *because* clause begins the sentence. Change sentences 2 and 4 so that the *because* clause ends the sentence.

1. Some companies say that businesses should not be involved in family matters because those matters are personal.

   Because _____

   _____

2. Because frustrated employees cannot focus on their work or careers, it makes sense for companies to offer family benefits.

   _____

   _____

3. Some companies are willing to address these issues because they don't want to risk losing their top talent.

   Because _____

   _____

4. Because recruiting and keeping good people is important to us, we have to fill their needs.

   _____

   _____

5. HBO provides someone to look after an employee's sick child at home because the company saves money by having the employee at work instead of having to hire a temporary.

   Because _____

   _____

   _____

VOCABULARY CHECK

The following words are used on the video. Which words are *used together*?
Match the words on the left with those on the right. When you finish
watch the video again and check your answers.

59:14–
01:03:50

1. _____ career	a. on investment
2. _____ redefined	b. alternative
3. _____ restructured	c. path
4. _____ child	d. turnover
5. _____ attract	e. new ground
6. _____ reduce	f. care
7. _____ improve	g. productivity
8. _____ break	h. benefits
9. _____ innovative	i. jobs
10. _____ return	j. better employees

CATEGORIZING WORDS

The words in the box are used on the video. Write each word under the
correct heading below.

account	earnings	expensive	flexible	innovative
investment	progressive	restructure	return	revolution

WORDS ASSOCIATED WITH CHANGES IN COMPANIES/CORPORATIONS	WORDS ASSOCIATED WITH MONEY
1. _____	_____
2. _____	_____
3. _____	_____
4. _____	_____
5. _____	_____

READING

Read the excerpts of the Associated Press article, "FSU study: Profits, not
people are more important." Then state the main idea and fill in the chart
that follows.

FSU STUDY: PROFITS, NOT PEOPLE ARE MORE IMPORTANT

Companies are tightening belts and bottom lines, and not worryingmuch about employees' satisfaction, human-resource managers say.

A tightening economy has forced U.S. companies to be more concerned with profit than with employee satisfaction and benefits, a Florida State University survey indicates.

Corporate personnel managers who traditionally have protected employees, now seem more concerned with looking out for the boss, the study, released Monday, showed.

"In the past, human-resource managers were the voice of the employee," said Florida State management professor Jack Fiorito. "I see that changing greatly. Things that don't directly cut costs or increase productivity are getting pushed to the back burner."

Fiorito, management professor William Anthony and assistant professor K. Michelle Kacmar asked 600 Florida human-resource managers to rate the workplace issues they were most concerned with today.

The managers represented companies in business and industries such as construction, sales, finance, manufacturing, utilities, education, public administration, hospitals and health care.

"A lot of firms consider issues they could address before as luxuries now," Anthony said. "Now they feel like they are fighting for their survival, which means they are focusing on things that will have a direct and immediate effect on the bottom line."

He said bloated management structures and international competition have forced most companies to reassess their priorities.

The researchers found the managers most concerned with health-care costs (99 percent rated it important or very important) and employee productivity (97 percent).

They were least concerned with providing jobs for spouses (43 percent), offering job-sharing opportunities (43 percent) and giving new fathers paternity leave (45 percent). The next lowest issues were care for the elderly (46 percent), helping employees relocate (50 percent) fetal protection from workplace hazards (53 percent) and flexible working hours (58 percent).

"Even though issues such as dual careers and flexible hours will make a company a better place to work, it's hard to put a dollar figure on them," Fiorito said. "They're hard to measure from a cost standpoint." . . .

Adapted and reprinted with permission of the *Associated Press*, from November 18, 1992 Tallahassee Democrat Business Section

1. Main Idea: _____

2. Workplace Issues managers rated as important or very important:

_____

WORKPLACE ISSUES	Rating Received*
a. Cutting health care costs	__ %
b. _____	97%
c. _____	58%
d. Fetal protection from workplace hazards	__ %
e. _____	50%
f. _____	46%
g. Giving new fathers parternity leave	__ %
h. _____	43%
i. _____	43%

*percent of managers who rated the issues important or very important.

DISCUSSION

Work in groups. Discuss the answers to the following questions.

1. Which view of business, that on the video or that in the article, is typical in your country?

2. Which view of business will become the trend in the 1990's? In the next century? Why?

3. What kinds of employee benefits and services should business companies or NOT provide for their employees? Why?

ROLE PLAY

Work in pairs. One student will play the role of the Human Resources Manager. The other student will play the role of the Employee Representative. Read the situation and the role descriptions below and decide who will play each role. After a ten-minute preparation, begin the problem-solving meeting.

THE SITUATION: **Management-Labor Problem-Solving Meeting**
A large company faces serious problems due to international competition and a recession. Wages have been frozen for two years, a factory has been closed, another may be closed soon, and some employees have been laid off. Meanwhile, top management continues to enjoy big salaries and other benefits. A meeting has

been called to discuss how management and labor can work together and solve the problems the company is facing.

ROLE DESCRIPTION: **Human Resource Manager**

You are the Human Resource Manager and are trying to help your CEO to cut costs and improve productivity in your company. While you wish the company could do more for its employees, including yourself, you feel strongly that the company is fighting for its survival and must get its workers to work harder and smarter for fewer benefits in order to prosper in the future. Prepare a list of key concerns that management has for the problem-solving meeting with the employee representative. Persuade the representative to agree with your ideas for action.

ROLE DESCRIPTION: **Employee Representative**

You have been selected by the employees to represent them in discussions with management about their concerns. While you understand that the company has gone through some tough times, you also realize that the top executives of the company are doing quite well and getting extra benefits at the same time that employee salaries have been frozen and some workers have been laid off. Prepare a list of employee concerns for the problem-solving meeting with the human resource manager. Persuade the manager to agree with your ideas for action.

WRITING

Complete one of the following activities.

1. As the human resource manager, write a 200-250 word executive summary to the CEO about the results of the meeting. Be sure to include the concerns of both sides, yours and the employee representative's, and the ideas for action that have been agreed upon. If you have space, also list the key areas of disagreement. Write this in a positive way, so that the CEO will think of you in a positive way.

2. As the employee representative, write a 200-250 word executive summary to the employees organization about the results of the meeting. Be sure to include the concerns of both sides, yours and the management's, and the ideas for action that have been agreed upon. If you have space, also list the key areas of disagreement. Write this in a positive way, so that the employees will think that you did a good job for them.

3. As a business consultant, write a 200-250 word executive summary to the CEO of a major company, listing what you think are the workplace trends of the next 10 years and why you think these trends will occur.

Segment 11

Computers and Consumers: User-Friendly or User-Surly?

From: Business World, 4/29/90
Begin: 01:04:19
Length: 5:21
Note: This segment is not closed captioned.

BEFORE YOU WATCH

TALKING POINTS

1. How have computers changed the way you live and work?
2. How have computers changed the way businesses operate in your country?
3. What problems have you, or people you know, had with computers?

PREDICTING

Work in groups. Based on the title of the news report and the questions above, predict the kinds of information you think will be included on the video.

1. _____
2. _____
3. _____
4. _____
5. _____

KEY WORDS

The *italicized* words in the sentences below will help you to understand the video. Study the sentences. Then write your own definition of each word.

1. The computer businesspeople use so much *jargon* when they talk that I don't understand what they are saying.

   jargon: _____

2. I was working on the computer for three hours and then suddenly had a *disk crash* that destroyed everything.

   disk crash: _____

3. One of the real advantages that the Apple MacIntosh had in the 1980's was that it was *user-friendly*.

   user-friendly: _____

4. The boss is an *advocate* of having the newest computers around the office; he thinks having new technology will improve productivity.

   advocate: _____

5. One big issue in using computers is *compatibility*. Will this software work well with that hardware or will there be problems?

   compatibility: _____

6. Many people need a lot of *training* before they become comfortable using new types of hardware and software.

   training: _____

7. Some people always keep a printed *back-up* copy of anything they put on the computer.

   back-up: _____

8. There can be a real *psychic cost* to computerization, especially for someone who is forced into a computing environment.

   psychic cost: _____

WHILE YOU WATCH

01:04:39-
01:09:29

GETTING THE MAIN IDEA

Watch the news report and listen for the answers to the following questions. Take brief notes on the answers. Then compare your answers with those of another student.

What are some problems that people have with computers?
How do most people **feel** when they have these problems?
What is the real **cause** of the problems?
How do some businesses **deal with** these problems ?

| What? |
| How/feel? |
| What/cause? |
| How/deal with? |

CHECKING YOUR PREDICTIONS

Look at your answers to the PREDICTING exercise on page 101. Look at the video again. Which kinds of information were actually included on the video?

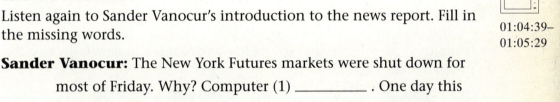

01:04:39–
01:09:29

WHAT'S MISSING?

Listen again to Sander Vanocur's introduction to the news report. Fill in the missing words.

01:04:39–
01:05:29

Sander Vanocur: The New York Futures markets were shut down for most of Friday. Why? Computer (1) _____ . One day this winter half the nation's long (2) _____ calls didn't get completed. Again, (3) _____ failure. Those are giant systems, but the same (4) _____ on a smaller scale are every day events. After all, there are an estimated (5) _____ million personal computers in use in the U.S. It's an industry that has revolutionized our lives, improving (6) _____ , employing directly or indirectly hundreds of thousand—one of the few industries in which the (7) ___ still leads the world.

But what about the other side of this (8) $_____ billion a year business, with its jargon of disk crashes and format failures, where computers seem more surly than (9) _____ , and where sometimes we're made to feel that when systems fail, the fault lies with the (10) _____ , not the makers. Just ask Mitch Kapor, the founder of Spreadsheet maker Lotus.

NOTETAKING

01:05:30– 01:06:31 Watch the next part of the video. Take brief notes on the answers to the following questions. Then compare your notes with those of another student.

1. According to Mitch Kapor, what is the secret shame of the PC industry?

   _____

2. According to Patricia Seybold, what do most people think when they have problems using their computers or software packages?

   _____

3. What does Patricia Seybold think the real problem is?

   _____

4. Why does Fred Davis, of PC Labs, get frustrated?

   _____

INFORMATION MATCH

01:06:32– 01:07:40 Watch the next part of the video. Match the businesses/people with the correct information. (One of the items below does not refer to any particular company but rather to the the business world generally. Leave that item blank.)

a. Bank of Boston   b. IBM   c. "PC" magazine   d. Stone & Webster
   (Ms. Proskauer)   (Mr. Machrone)   (Mr. Orenstein)

1. _____ Recalled its $500 add-in card because it was destroying data.

2. _____ Feels the biggest overall issue is compatibility.

3. _____ Uses PC's for everything from design to travel planning to document storage.

4. _____ Has 1,200 PC's.

5. _____ Annual costs per microcomputer range between $6,000 and $18,000.

6. _____ 80% of the time in training is spent on 20% of the function of the software package.

WHO'S WHO?

01:07:41– 01:08:44 Look at the chart below. Then watch the video and check (✔) the appropriate boxes. You may need to watch the video several times to complete the exercise.

Who. . .?	Ronnie Davis	Chuck Eisler
1. is a small business owner		
2. is a theatrical producer		
3. uses an Apple Macintosh computer		
4. uses a Compaq computer		
5. had a 24-page proposal go to "Data Heaven"		
6. experienced failure with a computer that held plans for a big dinner party		
7. now keeps a printed back-up copy of everything		
8. has thought of going back to using longhand, typewriters, and calculating machines		

TRUE OR FALSE?

Watch the next part of the video. Are the following statements *true* or *false*? Write **T** (true) or **F** (false). Make the false statements true by changing one or two words.

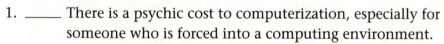

01:08:45–
01:09:29

1. _____ There is a psychic cost to computerization, especially for someone who is forced into a computing environment.

2. _____ The insurance benefits analysts were happy after their work was computerized.

3 _____ John Hancock faced hardware failures, unplugged systems, and many other problems.

4. _____ John Hancock was well prepared for the calls and problems that happened.

LANGUAGE POINT: PHRASAL VERBS

The excerpts below are from the video. Complete each sentence with one of the phrasal verbs in the box. *Be sure to change the verb tense if necessary.* When you finish, watch the video again and check your answers.

crop up	figure out	get . . .out
go back to	pick up	shut down

1. The New York Futures markets were ___*shut down*___ for most of Friday.

2. There's something wrong with me because I can't _____ how to make this machine work.

3. Still, Davis reports only product performance, not necessarily how long it takes to _____ it _____ of the box and get it running right.

4. We did the party by _____ the telephone and saying . . ."

5. There were moments of thinking about maybe _____ longhand and typewriters and calculating machines. . . .

6. . . . I don't think we were really quite prepared for the deluge of calls and problems that were going to _____ .

VOCABULARY CHECK: EXPRESSIONS

The following sentences are from the video. What do the expressions in *italics* mean? Circle the answer that is closest in meaning.

1. So there's this *conspiracy of silence* that PC's, despite all the wonderful things that they could do . . . for the average person are still frustratingly difficult to use. . .

   a. protest
   b. absence of protest
   c. group decision to not say
   d. group decision to say

2. I think consumers are somewhat *up the creek without a paddle*. I hate to say it and I wish it weren't so.

   a. in trouble with no one to help
   b. complaining too much about products
   c. lazy and not willing to learn more about products
   d. independent

3. Why such a *sorry state of affairs*? It's part hardware, part software.

   a. willingness to apologize
   b. bad situation
   c. lack of good equipment
   d. low level of activity

4. When a computer holding the plans for a *sit-down dinner* failed, it was a recipe for disaster.

   a. family dinner
   b. formal dinner party
   c. fast-food party
   d. late night supper

5. "Pardon me, I hate to bother you with this, but my computer *is down*, and we just can't recall what time we're serving the salmon . . ."

   a. is not working
   b. is reduced in price
   c. is gone
   d. is on the floor

6. There were moments of thinking about maybe going back to longhand and typewriters and calculating machines, (you know) that there was some *saving grace* in those after all.

   a. cost efficiency
   b. worthwhile benefit
   c. elegance
   d. waste time

7. John Hancock found *its hands full* when it tried to computer train its entire insurance sales force.

   a. it discovered a good idea
   b. it had an easy job
   c. it became very busy
   d. it had a lot of time

8. Hardware failures, unplugged systems, *you name it, the whole gamut*, and I don't think we were really quite prepared. . .

   a. every type of computer system
   b. anything related to computer hardware
   c. anything related to computer software
   d. the whole range of possible problems

DISCUSSION

Work in groups. Discuss your answers to the following questions.

1. Do you advise people to make printed back-up copies of important information they put on the computer? Why or why not?

2. How should businesses change how people work, if at all, because of computers and other new technology?

3. How will work situations in the future be similar to those of today? How will they be different? Explain your answers.

ROLE PLAY

Work in pairs. One student will play the role of the manager. The other student will play the role of the employee. Read the situation and the role descriptions below and decide who will play each role. After a ten-minute preparation, begin the informal meeting.

THE SITUATION: **An Informal Manager-Employee Meeting**

Everyone in a large company has been working very hard for a long time. Business is good, but one recent problem is that many employees are unhappy working with computers so much. A few have quit and gone to work for other companies that give them more freedom in structuring their work and using computers. One employee has asked for an informal meeting with the manager to discuss the working situation.

ROLE DESCRIPTION: **Manager**

You are a manager in charge of 30 workers. They have been working with you for a long time and are generally doing good jobs, though you often think that your section could get more work done if people would learn to use their computers more and talk to each other less. Prepare a list of possible changes or guidelines for employees. You might, or might not, want to mention these in the meeting with the employee.

ROLE DESCRIPTION: **A Tired Employee**

You are an employee who has worked for this manager for two years. You feel that you are a very hard worker and are proud of your work, but lately you've been feeling tired and depressed. Your eyesight is getting worse and you're having headaches. One of your co workers recently quit for the same reasons and joined a company which gives employees more freedom in structuring their work and lets some people work at home two days a week. Prepare a list of things you would like to change about your job and include reasons for the changes. Persuade your boss that the changes will be good for you and the company.

READING

Read the excerpts of the article from The Economist, "White-collar computers." Then fill in the grid that follows.

WHITE-COLLAR COMPUTERS

Businesses are seeking more help from intelligent machines.
Ideally, machines and human beings should each do what they are good at.

Every customer has at least one horror story to tell of a company or a government department that is unable to stop sending wrong bills, or to correct an address, or to divulge a piece of information "because of the computer". ... So the very thought of giving machines more responsibilities will send chills down many spines. Fear not. Companies are finding that the more intelligent machines are allowed to play to their strengths, the more they reduce human obstinacy.

Intelligent machines are increasingly being used to hide the brain-numbing complexity of modern business's products and processes, letting people concentrate on customers. In addition, to providing better service, this redistribution of work should give new (and unsexist) meaning to the phrase "man's work".

One of the most ambitious efforts to employ intelligent machines is being undertaken in the credit-card operations of American Express. The firm is building a "knowledge highway" in which bright computers will help people with every step of the job of managing credit, from card applications to collecting overdue accounts. The business goal is to use the machines to shield both credit-card holders and employees from the bureaucracy needed to manage American Express's vast business—so leaving employees free to devote their efforts to building relationships with customers.

The machines help in several ways. The latest addition to the "knowledge highway" is designed to help with overdue accounts. It leaves humans in charge of collection, but protects them from error at every step. The system automatically pulls together all of the information needed to analyze an account. Previously analysts had to make 22 queries on average—to computers spread across the whole of the company—each time they looked at a problem account. Now they typically make only one. The computer keeps track of which state or national laws might affect the account. It helps to generate a dunning letter. It files all the paperwork. And it automatically reminds the analyst if the account needs to be looked at again.

Thanks to such automated assistance, American Express is gradually changing the sorts of people it recruits to manage credit. Instead of hiring people good at number-crunching and applying complex rules, it is turning to people who know how to deal with people. And it is giving them more scope to use their skills. Previously the sheer complexity of the work meant that jobs had to be narrowly defined in order to be manageable. With that complexity largely hidden, American Express reckons it can define jobs more broadly—so giving generalists more freedom to make their customers happy.

American Express is not alone. . . . Compaq, a maker of personal computers, is trying to improve its customer service by installing automated assistants that work on the principle that reasoning is often just a matter of remembering the best precedent. Using "case-based reasoning" technology from Inference, one of the leading suppliers of artificial intelligence software, Compaq is building a compendium of the problems that customers have had with its personal computers and the solutions which Compaq has come up with...

In every case, the key to making these intelligent technologies work is to build them into the structure of the organization. That can be expensive...
But only with tight integration can companies redistribute work between people and machines.

That redistribution can bring dangers as well as benefits. By hiding unavoidable complexity from human view, machine intellect certainly enables people to do more work. But it can also make them more tolerant of needless complexity. Someday someone will inevitably go too far. Bankers, for example, are talking about using artificial intelligence to enable their people to sell financial products too varied and sophisticated for the salesmen to understand. Now that is an intelligent idea that could leave someone looking very stupid indeed.

©1992, The Economist Newspaper Group, Inc., Edited and reprinted with permission, 8/1/92, pp. 57–58.

1. Examples of how computers have caused problems for customers:

   a. _____   c. _____

   b. _____

2. One example of how computers are helping business:

   a. Company: _____

   b. Name of idea: _____

   c. Purpose of idea: _____

   d. Ways computers can help with overdue accounts:

      1 _____   5 _____

      2 _____   6 _____

      3 _____   7 _____

      4 _____

   e. Change in recruitment because of the computer:

      _____

3. Another example of how computers are helping business:

   a. Company: _____

   b. Objective: _____

   c. How: _____

   d. Reason for using the computer: _____

4. The key to making intelligent technologies work:

   _____

5. What is a possible danger of doing this?

   a. _____

   b. _____

WRITING

Complete one of the following activities.

1. You work for a company that could use new technology to improve the way it does business. Write an executive summary, 200-250 words, recommending what to get, why it will help the company, and how it will work.

2. You have strong views about the wave of new technology that is changing the way people work and live and the way that businesses are managed. Write a letter to the editor of the local newspaper, telling why the new techology is good (or bad) and what should be done about it. Use examples to illustrate your ideas.

Segment 12
Sharing Sweet Success

From: 20/20, 5/22/92
Begin: 01:09:43
Length: 12:87

BEFORE YOU WATCH

TALKING POINTS

Work in groups. Discuss your answers to the following questions.

1. How important is it for a company to have a basic philosophy, or basic idea of its purpose and way of doing business?

2. If you had your own company, what would your basic philosophy be?

3. If you had your own company, what would you do in order to 'work smart'? Be as specific as you can be.

PREDICTING

Work in groups. Based on the title of the news report and the questions above, write down three questions you think will be answered on the video.

1. _____

2. _____

3. _____

KEY WORDS

The *italicized* words in the sentences below will help you understand the video. Study the sentences. Then match the words with the meanings.

1. Unfortunately, the country's economic growth continues to be *sluggish*.

2. Some would say that every company should have a *social mission*, for example, to help people in the community; others say that a company's mission should just be to earn as much profit as possible.

3. She is a *shrewd* businessperson; she would never make such a careless mistake.

4. The CEO still has the *ideals* of his youth, that is, he still wants to do good things.

5. He is a marketing genius; he has an *uncanny instinct* for how each product should be sold in each market. He always succeeds.

6. The company keeps on being more and more successful. It has reported *record earnings* for three straight years.

7. He is a small investor, but he does own some *stock* in IBM, and GM.

8. The CEO has an *obsession* about quality and flexibility. He says we absolutely must have the top quality all the time and must also be ever flexible in adapting to market trends.

9. They are saving up their money in order to buy a fast-food *franchise*.

10. The CEO *integrates* various functions of the business. For example, he wants marketing people to work very closely all the time with production people and financial people.

1. _____ *sluggish*	a.	constant and total motivation
2. _____ *social mission*	b.	clever, smart
3. _____ *shrewd*	c.	more money received than ever before
4. _____ *ideals*	d.	slower than normal
5. _____ *uncanny instinct*	e.	belief in doing something for the community
6. _____ *record earnings*	f.	brings different things together, to form a whole
7. _____ *stock*	g.	extraordinary, natural feeling
8. _____ *obsession*	h.	business arrangement in which people pay a large company for the right to own and manage a local store of the same name
9. _____ *franchise*	i.	principles or ideas that seem good
10. _____ *integrates*	j.	ownership share in a company

GETTING THE MAIN IDEA

Watch the news report and listen for the answers to the following questions. Take brief notes on the answers. Then compare your answers with those of another student.

01:10:06–
01:23:23

> **Who** is doing **what, where**?
> **Why** and **how** are they doing this?

Who?	
What?	
Where?	
Why?	
How?	

CHECKING YOUR PREDICTIONS

Look at the questions you wrote in the PREDICTING exercise on page 111. Which of your questions are answered on the video? What answers are given?

01:10:06–
01:23:23

WHAT'S MISSING?

Listen again to Hugh Downs' introduction to the news report. Fill in the missing words.

01:10:42–
01:11:16

Hugh Downs: How much money do you make, compared to your
(1) _____ ? In recent months, there have been numerous
(2) _____ highlighting the sometimes enormous gap
between (3) _____ and workers on the line and other
stories about workers (4) _____ _____ , considered disposable in a
sluggish (5) _____ . Well, tonight, Bob Brown introduces us
to a couple of extremely successful businessmen who take a totally
(6) _____ approach. They spread the wealth and they
take care of their (7) _____ and the community. In fact,
at Ben & Jerry's 8) _____ _____ , everybody's troubles seem to
melt away.

WHAT DO YOU SEE?

Watch the next part of the video with the *sound off*. Number the following items from 1 to 7 in the order in which you see them. The first one has been done for you.

_____ A sign that reads "Ben and Jerrys"

_____ A picture of cows on the side of a building

_____ A sign that reads "To make the world a better place"

_____ A picture of the planet earth on the side of a building

__1__ An icicle

_____ A sign that reads "Leave no child behind"

_____ A sign that reads "Take action here"

NOTETAKING

Watch the beginning of the video again, from just after the introduction, and take brief notes on the answers to the following questions. Then compare your notes with those of another student.

1. Where is Ben & Jerry's located?

   _____

2. What is sinful about their ice cream?

   _____

3. What is the two-part bottom line of the company?

   _____ and _____

4. What kind of ice cream does the company make?

   _____

5. What is the company market share of that market?

   _____ %

6. What are the market share rankings for these companies:

   Kraft Foods' Frusen Gladje ____

   Pillsbury's Haagen Dazs ____

   Ben & Jerry's ____

7. What new product line is Ben & Jerry's promoting heavily?

   _____

8. a. What will this year's sales be?

   _____

   b. How much more is that from four years ago?

   _____

9. How much did last year's stock increase? _____ %

10. How much did the company earn last year? $ _____

11. What is Ben & Jerry's obsession?

    _____

12. How does the company market its products?

    _____

TRUE OR FALSE?

Watch the next part of the video. Are the following statements *true* or *false*? Write **T** (true) or **F** (false). Make the false statements true by changing one or two words.

01:18:10–
01:21:03

1. _____ Because of the enormous growth of the company in the last 10 years, Ben & Jerry have to keep most of the responsibility for the daily business operations.

2. _____ Anyone who takes a managerial job at Ben & Jerry's knows that they can become extremely rich if they do well.

3. _____ The highest paid executives in the U.S. take home salaries that are no more than seven times the salary of the lowest paid worker.

4. _____ No executive at Ben & Jerry's is currently earning more than $100,000 a year.

5. _____ Employees at Ben & Jerry's feel valued because they are treated like they are important.

6. _____ In 1990, Ben & Jerry's had to pay more than $3,000 fines to the government for creating too much ice cream waste around their plant.

7. _____ One of Ben & Jerry's solutions for dealing with ice cream waste was to set up a farmer with a herd of pigs because pigs can eat the waste.

8. _____ Ben believes that the company does business in a way that integrates community concerns with those of making a profit.

CHECKING WHAT YOU HEAR

Watch the final part of the video and check (✔) the statements that you hear.

01:21:04–
01:22:23

1. ☐ Why didn't you bring back samples for your friends?

2. ☐ You'd get sick if I did that.

3. ☐ How do they still manage to do business when more and more people want low-fat or non-fat frozen desserts?

4. ☐ Well, they've gone heavily into frozen yogurt products now.

5. ☐ It's lucky that they went to Vermont.

6. ☐ How did they get started in the first place?

7. ☐ They'd known each other since college.

8. ☐ They looked for college towns with no homemade ice cream stores and the only one they could find was in Vermont.

9. ☐ They went to a converted gas station there, opened an ice cream store and the rest is history.

10. ☐ I've lost a pound and a half just listening to you.

AFTER YOU WATCH

LANGUAGE POINT: STATING GOALS & OBJECTIVES

On the video, Bob Brown mentions Ben & Jerry's "social mission that defines what . . .(they) want their company to stand for."

Here are four similar ways of stating goals or objectives
a. Our mission is to . . .
b. Our goal is to . . .
c. Our objective is to . . .
d. Our purpose is to . . .

State goals based on the following situations. Introduce each statement with expression a, b, c, or d, as indicated.

Example: State the goal of tripling earnings in five years. (c)

Our objective is to triple earnings in five years.

1. State the goal of making profits and helping the community at the same time. (a)

   _____

2. State the goal of improving communication between management and employees. (d)

   _____

3. State the goals of reducing product defects, improving productivity, and increasing sales. (c)

   _____

4. State the goal of becoming the top company in market share. (b)

_____

5. State the goal of making the best products possible at the lowest possible cost. (any)

_____

VOCABULARY CHECK: IDIOMS

The following sentences are from the video. What do the idioms in *italics* mean? Circle the answer that is closest in meaning.

1. Children are indoctrinated by signs of the social mission that defines what Ben Cohen & Jerry Greenfield want their company to *stand for*.
   a. believe in
   b. talk about
   c. be known for
   d. defend itself against

2. Even though they don't *look the part*, they are shrewd businessmen.
   a. analyze data
   b. study the bottom line
   c. appear to be so
   d. take care of details

3. They have managed to *live up to* both their ideals and their stockholders.
   a. pretend to work with
   b. try to do well according to
   c. be successful by compromising
   d. earn a living from

4. If there's one area where Ben & Jerry's is *strictly business*, it is an obsession with quality control.
   a. only concerned about making money
   b. focused only on the work
   c. a problem area that needs working on
   d. generous about profits

5. Ben and Jerry have *turned over* most of the responsibility for daily business operations to a senior management team...
   a. been forced to give
   b. given
   c. thought about giving
   d. given and then taken back

6. The senior management team also *stays aligned with* the values on which the company was founded.
   a. operates upon
   b. keeps changing
   c. ignores
   d. adapts where necessary

7. Sensitive to diet research that shows fat is bad, they have now *gone heavily into* frozen yogurt products.
   a. make and sell a lot of
   b. bought other companies that make
   c. cut old product lines and replaced them with
   d. reduced production of

8. They tried a series of odd jobs and neither one of them *made it*, so they said, "Well, let's open a homemade ice cream shop."
   a. produced anything worthwhile
   b. could work well with their hands
   c. became successful
   d. earned a salary

DISCUSSION

Work in groups. Discuss your answers to the following questions.

1. What do you think about the way Ben Cohen and Jerry Greenfield run their business? How would you run their company differently?

2. If you were the CEO of your own company, what goals would you have for the managing employees? For dealing with suppliers? For pursuing quality? For competing with your competitors? For dealing with customers? For handling stockholders? For interacting with the community? For protecting the environment? For any other concerns you have?

3. Why would you choose these goals over others you might choose?

ROLE PLAY

Work in pairs. Read the situation and the role descriptions below and decide who will play each role. After a ten-minute individual preparation, begin the role play.

THE SITUATION: **Meeting to Establish a New Company**

Two old friends have decided to discuss the possibility of becoming partners in a new business. There is much to decide on if the idea is to become a reality, for example, the type of business, how they will get capital to start the business, how they will work together, how they will make decisions on finance, daily operations, marketing, etc.

ROLE DESCRIPTION: **Student A's Name**

You are excited by the idea of becoming partners with your friend in a new business. Prepare your ideas on the kind of business you would like to start, how you can get capital for the start-up, and how you can work together. Also prepare questions about how you will run the business on a day-to-day basis and about various functional areas, such as marketing, production, etc. You may need to persuade your friend that this is a great idea.

ROLE DESCRIPTION: **Student B's Name**

You like the idea of becoming partners with your friend, but you are not sure that this idea will work. Prepare a list of questions about what kind of business it would be, how finances would be handled, who would do what, how problems and disagreements would be resolved, etc. Although you are not sure that this is a good move, prepare a few business ideas that you might like to explore with your friend.

READING

Read the excerpts from the article, "The Caring Company," from *The Economist* and then answer the questions that follow.

THE CARING COMPANY

A strong corporate culture is said to help firms succeed. Does it?

Management thinkers have long associated a strong corporate culture—the beliefs, goals, and values that guide the behavior of a firm's employees—with superior long-term performance. The theory is that strong cultures can help workers march to the same drummer; create high levels of employee loyalty and motivation; and provide the company with structure and controls, without the need for an innovation-stifling bureaucracy.

In a new book, *Corporate Culture and Performance*, published by Free Press, John Kotter and James Heskett, report on their four year study to examine the link between corporate culture and economic performance. To do this, the authors calculated "culture-strength indices" for over 200 big American firms. Companies such as Wal-Mart, J.P. Morgan and Proctor & Gamble scored highest; bankrupt, but still operating, American Airlines scored among the worst.

The authors then tried to calculate the strength of the firms' cultures with their economic performance over an 11 year period. Their analysis did show a positive correlation between strong cultures and long-term economic performance, but it was a weaker association than most management theorists would have expected. Strong-cultured firms seemed almost as likely to perform poorly as their weak-cultured rivals. The popular view that a strong corporate culture invariably leads to success, they concluded, was "just plain wrong".

What is it about the cultures of the high-performing companies that makes them successful? The authors' theory is that firms whose cultures seem consistently to produce long-term economic success share one fundamental characteristic: their managers do not let the short-term interests of shareholders override all else, but care equally about all of the company's "stakeholders".

Over the long-term, mind you, the authors believe that these interests converge. "Only when managers care about the legitimate interests of shareholders do they strive to perform well economically over time, and in a competitive industry that is only possible when they take care of their customers, and in a competitive labor market that is only possible when they take care of those who serve customers—employees."

One snag is that the right corporate culture, reckons the authors, often takes decades to evolve. The best way to speed this up, they say, may be to appoint a boss who is either unconventional or an outsider and preferably both. Nonconformists and outsiders are good at shaking up, or creating corporate cultures. Just don't expect any results this century.

©1992, *The Economoist Newspaper Group, Inc.*, Edited and reprinted with permission, 6/6/92, p. 75.

1. Management thinkers have long associated strong corporate culture with _____

2. Corporate culture = _____

3. Reasons for the theory: _____

    _____

4. What conclusion did John Kotter and James Heskett reach?

    _____

5. The one fundamental characteristic of cultures of high-performing companies: _____

6. Three key groups that management is concerned with:

    1 _____   2 _____   3 _____

7. One problem with getting the right corporate culture:

    _____

8. The best way to deal with this problem is to:

    _____

WRITING

Complete one of the following activities.

1. Write a short report, 250-300 words, on how Ben & Jerry's Ice Cream Company has developed and has used a strong corporate culture to work smart and achieve good results. Analyze this culture and predict what effect it will have on the company's success in the future.

2. Pick any two companies you know about and write a short report, 250-300 words, describing, discussing, and comparing their corporate cultures in terms of characteristics and effect on economic performance.

Wal-Mart vs. Brattleboro

from *Business World*, August 23, 1992

Announcer: From ABC News, this is *Business World*. Now from New York here's Stephen Aug.

Stephen Aug: The Goliath of retailing, Wal-Mart, the empire of the late Sam Walton founded 30 years ago this summer, is now the nation's largest retailer. And even the recession hasn't slowed its relentless march towards new stores and higher earnings. One key to Wal-Mart's success has been its focus on small and mid-size America. Cities and towns largely ignored by other major chain stores. But while Wal-Mart's coming may be welcomed by shoppers, it's often the shadow of doom for local merchants the Davids in its path.

(voice over) At the foot of Mount Monadnock, part of Wal-Mart's New Hampshire expansion is taking root. But the nearest community is not in New Hampshire, it's Brattleboro, Vermont. And while Brattleboro won't benefit from the tax revenue, it will have to cope with the added traffic. Wal-Mart shoppers will have to pass through this congested intersection and cross a two-lane bridge to get to the store.

Lea Stewart, *Brattleboro Food Co-op*: This is a really old town, a small town. Main street is very narrow, and it could become a nightmare, so we really have to see how we're really going to help the flow of traffic.

Stephen Aug: *(voice over)* But of course, traffic is not the only concern. According to a study conducted in Iowa, about 60% of a Wal-Mart's sales come at the expense of local businesses.

Kenneth Stone, *Iowa State University*: We see a gigantic leakage away from such stores as hardware stores, men's clothing stores, variety stores, those types of stores that are competing directly with Wal-Mart.

Stephen Aug: *(voice over)* For the past five years, economist Kenneth Stone has been studying the impact that Wal-Mart has had on small towns in his home state of Iowa. The Brattleboro chamber of commerce invited Stone to deliver a wake-up call to local merchants.

Kenneth Stone: You can't go below them on these price-sensitive type items. You're better off staying a little bit above them because they, uh, won't—they'll leave you alone then. But once you go below them, the local manager has what? He or she has the authority to automatically go below you the minute they catch you below them.

Stephen Aug: *(voice over)* And in Iowa, there were some surprising victims of deep discounts.

Kenneth Stone: In the grocery business, we have lost 787 grocery stores in our state in the last decade—40 percent.

Stephen Aug: *(voice over)* The reason?

Kenneth Stone: Visualize your supermarket. How many aisles are health and beauty aids, cleaning supplies, paper products, pet supplies, so on and so forth? According to my figures, in my state it's nearly one third of the purchases in a standard grocery store are non-food items. So what happens when these super discount stores come in? People keep going to grocery stores to buy food but they merely slip over many items to the Wal-Mart store to buy the non-food items.

Stephen Aug: *(voice over)* But Brattleboro might prove the exception. The local grocery, for example, is a food co-op where shoppers are members and are willing to pay a little more for organically-grown, environmentally-sensitive products. And while local merchants understand they cannot compete on price, many are banking on customer service.

Nancy Hagstrom, *Newton Office Products*: When a consumer brings a product to us that he's bought at a Wal-Mart, like a fax machine, and has spent hours trying to learn how to run it, he's already very, very frustrated. We spend the time to teach them how to operate the machine and the next time they are looking for a product, they'll remember that they could avoid that frustration if they came to us first.

Stephen Aug: *(voice over)* At Sam's department store, which opened in 1932, customers help themselves to popcorn and pants are hemmed for free.

Stanley Borofsky, President, *Sam's Department Store*: We may take advantage of their hours. In other words, I think we're going to adjust our hours and try to stay open at the same time they are.

Stephen Aug: *(voice over)* Brown and Roberts has been in Brattleboro for 22 years. They offer everything from kitchen ware to hardware. And for local residents, credit is available.

Bernard Putnam, *Brown & Roberts*: It's bound to make a difference but I don't know. We'll just have to wait and see what happens.

Stephen Aug: *(voice over)* The river that divides New Hampshire from Vermont and Wal-Mart from Main Street is less than a mile. But with no sales tax on the New Hampshire side, discounts will be even deeper and harder for Vermont merchants to match because they have a five percent sales tax. At BRW Electronics, they're hoping that local residents will look beyond the savings.

Richard Harper, *Manager, BRW Electronics*: The realities are that when you buy at home, the dollars stay at home, the dollars get recirculated six or seven times. Very, very critical for a tax base here in this town and for this community to be healthy and successful.

Stephen Aug: And, by some estimates, by the end of this century, Wal-Mart may not only be the nation's largest retailer but its largest corporation as well.

Announcer: *Business World* is a presentation of ABC News. More Americans get their news from ABC News than from any other source.

TRANSCRIPT 2

New Trends in Retailing
from *Business World*, April 7, 1991

Announcer: From ABC News this is Business World with Sander Vanocur and Stephen Aug. Now from New York, here's Sander Vanocur.

Sander Vanocur, *ABC News*: The engine that drives the American economy is consumer spending. In 1990, American consumers spent $1.8 trillion retail dollars. Shopping in the U.S. had almost become a national pastime. The motto, "Shop till you drop," echoed through the malls. In the period 1980 to 1990, the number of shopping centers went up by 66 percent, while the population increased by only 10 percent, but there's a sea change under way in shopping habits. Retail space is going begging and, even if consumers do start spending again, their money is going in new directions. This week, our program will focus on the change in retailing: who's losing, who's winning, as the retail shopping spree that characterized the decade ends and consumers who once looked toward the top of the line now focus on the bottom line.

(voice over) Like many baby-boomers raising children, Nancy Gabriel says she no longer shops as she once did.

Nancy Gabriel, *teaching assistant:* Before, I used to go in, and style or color was a major thing. Now, price is really one of the first things I do look at.

Sander Vanocur: *(voice over)* With mounting family expenses, the Gabriels put discretion back in their discretionary spending.

Bill Gabriel, *manager:* We put several additions on a house and made improvements to the house. Now, as kids are starting to go into college and getting ready for college, we can't do things like that any longer. I've known people who have blown their whole retirement income on colleges, so from that perspective I'm concerned.

Sander Vanocur: *(voice over)* And they're willing to travel for bargains. One place high on their list is BJ's—a membership-only, no-frills wholesale club.

Bill Gabriel: We do basically shop in discount stores. I do not go to retail stores and shop. I hate to say that, but it's true.

Herbert Zarkin, *President, BJ's Wholesale Club:* The membership concept is one that you feel you're willing to become a committed, dedicate member. We don't want a person to come in and just be a casual shopper once in a while. We want you to come in and spend a large sum of money on a fairly routine basis.

Sander Vanocur: *(voice over)* That's because they need to turnover a large volume of goods since they operate on a margin of about 8 to 10 percent compared to 30 percent for a typical department store. Wholesale clubs aren't the only merchants giving department stores a run for their money. Catalog sales, television shopping, and shopping by computer are all gaining popularity, but the biggest challenge comes from discount stores, specialty shops that narrowly target a specific customer, category killers, giant discounters that sell one type of item like office supplies, and outlet stores where manufacturers sell their goods direct to the public.

Peter Siris, *Vice President, UBS Securities:* You're finding two things happening, one is consumers spending less, and then consumers also trading down. You know, they say, "You know, it's great to go into a glitzy, fancy store, and here's somebody playing a grand piano, but the fact of the matter is if I drive two miles to a warehouse club I can save five bucks, and I'd rather save five bucks than listen to the grand piano."

Sander Vanocur: *(voice over)* Siris says this reflects both a sobering economy and, perhaps, even more significant, long-term demographic trends. Once entrenched in middle age, every generation spends less and saves more. That was true in 1977, when the ratio of debt to income dropped like a rock from the under-35 to the over-65's, and it was true in 1988 as well. And debt-stressed baby boomers, hung over from the heady 80's, are less inclined to buy on impulse. In the mid-80's, Cattiva dresses were made to sell in department stores for about $500. Now they're made to sell for half that price.

Chuck Schwartz, *President, Cattiva:* People have become much more conservative. People are watching what they spend. People are watching for investment clothing more so than fads, and the dollar has become very precious.

Sander Vanocur: *(voice over)* Recognizing the men are becoming reluctant to replenish their wardrobes, Godfry's of Ohio, an independent store catering to executives, has taken drastic measures. Not only do they make house calls, they follow-up purchases with phone calls.

Drew Cashmere, *Executive Vice President, Godfry's:* We tend to find a lot of little problems that most men won't tell us initially, but we find it's really helped our business. We've gotten a lot of compliments.

Sander Vanocur: *(voice over)* With independents offering extra service and bare-bone, cost-cutting operations proliferating, traditional retailers are in trouble. After 87 years in southern California, Buffams, which operated 16 stores employing 1,300 people, is the latest venerable institution to join the casualty list.

John Duncan, *CEO, Buffams:* It's really a discount mode that the customer is looking for today. So having someone meet you at the front door and making sure you got treated properly in the store, make sure the clothes fit you properly, and that you know what you are buying—those days are disappearing for the mass of customer.

Sander Vanocur: That's it for this week. What ever business you're in we hope the week ahead is a prosperous one. I'm Sander Vanocur. On behalf of everyone here at *Business World*, thanks for being with us.

Announcer: *Business World* is a presentation of ABC News. More Americans get their news from ABC News than from any other source.

TRANSCRIPT 3

Too Many Tires

from *20/20*, April 8, 1988

Announcer: On the ABC News Magazine *20/20*, with Hugh Downs and Barbara Walters. You're looking at the world's biggest tire graveyard. Over 40 million of them on a California farm. They stink when they burn, take centuries to decay,–so how can we get rid of them? John Stossel–with some new solutions for too many tires!

Barbara Walters: It's probably not on anyone's wish list, but you're about to see what a pile of 40 million tires looks like. And while that sounds like a lot, it's only a fraction of the number of tires Americans have thrown away. Since the time of the Model T, we've discarded 2 billion tires. We add 200 million more each year and what on earth are we supposed to do with them? And where on earth? Well, someone has to worry about these things and around here we've nominated John Stossel.

Commercial Announcer #1: Tracks like an arrow, drinks up the water and spits out the miles, and that's—miles of smiles. . .

Commercial announcer #2: It'll go anywhere. Wrangler. One good reason why Goodyear outsells all the foreign radials combined.

John Stossel: *(voice over)* They look so good in the commercials but it doesn't take long before you're at some tire dealership or gas station saying, Take it off. I need a new one." And what does the gas station do with the old ones? Well, often they just take them out back and dump them somewhere. (on camera) So, most gas stations around the country end up with piles of used tires like this one. And what can they do with it? They can't take the tires to the local landfill. What if you tried to take them down to the country dump?

Bob Boydston, *Westley Triangle Truck Stop:* Well, they'd have a heart attack right on the spot, you know? They'd say, "Whoa!" I've—I've tried it. The same dumps that I used to dump in no longer accepts my tires.

John Stossel: *(voice over)* Why not? Well, for one thing, landfills are running out of room and even those that have room don't like tires because, well, tires are forever or almost forever. Most paper garbage, when exposed to sun and water, decomposes. In several years or so, it's dust. A rubber tire is a rubber tire for hundreds of years. To make things worse, they don't stay buried, they tend to creep back up to the surface. And to make things much worse, piles of tires can catch fire. Lightening started this fire at a stockpile outside Denver. It burned 6 days. The smoke could be seen as far away as Nebraska. And if you've ever smelled burning rubber, you know that seeing the smoke wasn't the problem. This is why landfills say, "No tires." And so all over the place there are smaller piles. People who just can find a legitimate way to get rid of old tires dump them. But now entrepreneurs are offering new solutions. In New Jersey, Metropolitan Tire Converters shreds tires and then sells the pieces to a company in Greece that somehow uses them as fuel. In Massachusetts, F & B enterprises cuts tires up and uses them to make nets for scallop fishing. And in Minnesota, the R.R.& E. Company grinds tires into powder and uses the powder to make things like carpet backing and hockey pucks. *(on camera)* But as far as solving the garbage problem, those steps aren't much help. Most of the country's tires just sit in piles like this one. And how big a problem is it? Well, pretty big, because all over the country there are monstrous ugly piles of tires. *(voice over)* This one, near Modesto, California, is the biggest. A cattle rancher owns the land. Twenty years ago he decided he wasn't making enough money on cattle so he told his neighbors, "I'll take your old tires if you give me ten cents per tire." They did and the word spread. Today, trucks collect tires from all over the region and dump thousands of tires every day—car tires, truck tires—now there are 40 million of them here. In places, the pile's 150 tires deep. I was a little nervous walking around here because rattlesnakes live in some of the tires. Apparently rattlesnakes are one of the few species that appreciates a 30-year-old tire. At any rate, there's no question that this is the biggest, ugliest pile of tires in the country. *(voice over)* A pile this big, however, does have an advantage: it seems to have inspired some people to do something about it. They're going to dump the tires into a huge incinerator and burn them. The heat from the fire they use to make electricity, enough to meet the energy needs of some 15,000 nearby homes. It makes sense: tires are made from oil. Why import oil when you have all these tires sitting around? One tire can heat one home for one day.

Gordon Marker, *Executive VP, Oxford Energy Co.***:** This is energy. People call it garbage.

John Stossel: *(voice over)* Gordon Marker of Oxford Energy is one of the engineers who's making it work.

Gordon Marker: Each one of these tires is 2-1/2 gallons of oil which can be created—transformed—into electrical energy.

John Stossel: *(voice over)* So here is private enterprise at its best, a factory that turns an eyesore into energy and expects to make a profit doing it. Makes me wonder *(voice over)* why isn't it done all over the country?

Gordon Marker: It should be done. It's not done here because nobody wants it in their backyard. I mean, we will wallow in our trash before we'll deal with it.

Barbara Walters: That's a lot of tires! Why don't other places do what Modesto, California did?

John Stossel: As he points out, it's the "not in my backyard" problem. The neighbors say, "Great idea, but not here."

Barbara Walters: Yeah, but does it smell? I mean, does it foul up the air?

John Stossel: Half the plant is pollution control equipment. It's been used in Germany now for 14 years. Here they just had testing in California, the air is clean. It works.

Barbara Walters: So people should follow the example.

John Stossel: I would think so. They're just about to give up on trying to build a plant in New Hampshire, however, because the local people said no.

Barbara Walters: Maybe this will change their minds.

John Stossel: Maybe.

Barbara Walters: Let us hope so. Thank you, John.

Hugh Downs: Well, that's *20/20* for tonight. We thank you for joining us.

Barbara Walters: And remember–we're in touch, so you be in touch. I'm Barbara Walters. . .

Hugh Downs: And I'm Hugh Downs

Barbara Walters: And for everyone here at ABC News, Goodnight.

Announcer: This has been the ABC News Magazine *20/20*.

TRANSCRIPT 4

Disney's Long-Term Strategies
from *Business World*, March 29, 1992

Announcer: From ABC News, this is *Business World*. Now from New York, here's Stephen Aug.

Stephen Aug: For the first time ever, an animated movie is up for the Oscar for Best Picture, Disney's "Beauty and the Beast." While Disney's been flying high on a string of movie hits, the company's long-term strategy relies heavily on revenues from its theme parks, where attendance has been down. Now, as ABC News correspondent Jim Bitterman reports, with its newest theme park only two weeks away from opening, Disney is betting that a French love affair with Mickey will be more than a fantasy.

Jim Bitterman: *(voice over)* At Disney's new entertainment complex, 20 miles east of Paris, an army of workers are rushing to beat the clock. They have to be finished on time, because Disney predicts more than 11 million people will want to visit the park before the end of the year. Analysts say visitors could even number as high as 13.5 million.

Robert Fitzpatrick, *President, Euro Disney:* I occasionally have a nightmare that all of France will decide to arrive at 9:01 on Sunday, April the 12th.

Jim Bitterman: *(voice over)* It is a legitimate fear. When the original Disneyland opened in California in 1955, overcrowding was so bad the first few days that people stayed away for months afterward. At Euro Disney, six hotels with 5 thousand rooms are waiting for the expected hordes. Inside the park, visitors will find the usual features of a Disneyland — Main Street, U.S.A., Frontier Land, Adventure Land, and Fantasy Land —all with a French accent. *(on camera)* Creating fantasy worlds has become something of a Disney trademark, but the real magic of Euro Disney is not so much the attractions as the imagination shown in the financing.

David Londoner, *Analyst, Wertheim Schroder:* It's probably the single best piece of project financing since the Suez Canal. Disney did an unbelievably good job of financing this. Put up an extraordinarily small amount of money — it's about $140 million — in a $4 billion project. They end up owning 49 percent of the equity.

Jim Bitterman: *(voice over)* The Walt Disney Company of California will also be the manager of the entire Euro Disney project, and gets a 3 percent management fee. As well, for the use of the Disney name, the U.S. company gets an additional 7.5 percent in royalties. But buyers of a special Euro Disney stock offering, who put up the bulk of the financing, don't get quite such a good deal.

Mr. Londoner: Disney California can earn as much as 50 percent of the cash flow, after those royalties, and after the other expenses, but before they split with the shareholders the remaining net income.

Jim Bitterman: *(voice over)* Euro Disney's president defends the terms.

Robert Fitzpatrick: I think it's important to note that the investment of the Walt Disney Company, when it first made the decision in September 1984, was by no means a sure thing.

Jim Bitterman: *(voice over)* That was also before Disney got the French government to give it major incentives, like extending a commuter line out to the project. And then there are the loan guarantees, the tax breaks, and the eventual construction of a special Euro Disney stop for France's high-speed train. Government officials declined to comment, but a local communist labor union representative says Disney used the threat of locating in Spain rather than France in order to drive a hard bargain.

Jean-Louis Chaumet, *Labor Representative, CGT: (through translator)* Disney put Barcelona and the French site in competition, and as a result of this bidding war, the French government won the contract at the expense of many laws and many hard-won social rights.

Jim Bitterman: *(voice over)* One right is how an employee dresses on the job. Disney's strict dress code has stirred up a controversy. At a Euro Disney recruitment drive in London, job seekers were shown this company video.

Narrator: *(Disney Company video)* One earring per ear, please. The diameter of the earring should be no bigger than two centimeters. Beards and mustaches are not part of the Disney look.

1st Job Seeker: It's a bit, like being at school, really, as far as I can see. I think they're going over the top, going for such a squeaky-clean American image.

2nd Job Seeker: What's unfair is they ask you to take your nose ring out. It's the smallest one I've got, and are they that strict?

Cowboy (on horseback): Ladies and gentlemen, permit me to introduce you to this congress of rough riders.

Jim Bitterman: *(voice over)* But the only exceptions to the all-American look are the real American cowboys and Indians, recruited for Buffalo Bill's Wild West show. They at least can have mustaches.

Disney Cowboy: These people are really fired up about the Old West and everything, and we're just giving them all we can, you know.

Jim Bitterman: *(voice over)* Still, some people complain that Disney is bringing what is disdainfully described here as "hamburger culture" to the land of haute culture.

Robert Fitzpatrick: Some of them have said, Well, Disney will endanger French culture," and I don't think of France as an old lady terrified of a mouse.

Jim Bitterman: *(voice over)* But will the Europeans buy all this? Disney is doing a marketing blitz just to make sure. A special store is already open to sell Euro Disney t-shirts and souvenirs. It even has a house-sized scale model of Sleeping Beauty's castle touring such unlikely places as eastern Europe. *(on camera)* And Disney's also expected to get European-wide television coverage of its opening day ceremonies—two hours of virtually free publicity in prime time, entirely under the control of Disney's own producers. [Mickey Mouse!]

(voice over) Yet no matter what happens after April 12th, financially the Disney Company will still come out a winner.

David Londoner: It's going to be very, very hard for Disney to lose anything on this thing. This has to be a total disaster, which it clearly will not be.

Jim Bitterman: *(voice over)* Jim Bitterman, ABC News, Paris.

Stephen Aug: That's it for this week. Whatever business you're in we hope the week ahead is a prosperous one. I'm Stephen Aug. On behalf of everyone here at *Business World*, thanks for being with us.

Announcer: *Business World* is a presentation of ABC News. More Americans get their news from ABC than any other source.

TRANSCRIPT 5

The International Airline Industry
from *Business World,* February 23, 1992

Announcer: From ABC News this is *Business World.* Now from New York, here's Forrest Sawyer.

Forrest Sawyer: Turbulence in the air; this past week the State Department issued an advisory, warning Americans about travelling in Europe, the Middle East and Africa. The reason: possible terrorism in the wake of the latest violence in the Middle East, another blow just as the airlines were hoping to recover from a disastrous 1991 brought on by the Gulf war and by recession, and punctuated by the failure of Pan Am and the bankruptcy of TWA. American carriers hoping to smooth out domestic bumps are turning to overseas routes for profits, but as Stephen Aug reports, there too, they could be in for a rough ride.

Stephen Aug: *(voice over)* As usual, Swissair flight 110 from Zurich arrived at New York's John F. Kennedy Airport on time. That's only one of the reasons some people prefer to fly European airlines.

Andrea Epstein, *American businessman:* The service is one very strong reason why we chose to fly Swissair. They're renowned for their excellent service.

Giovanni Conte, *Italian businessman:* Reliability is definitely the most important thing.

Stewart McLaughain, *American tourist:* I had flown Swissair before and found it to be great and they serve great chocolate and that's why we're back.

Stephen Aug: *(voice over)* But the Europeans are waking up to the fact that they will have to do more than hand out candy if they're to remain competitive.

Peter Leuthi, *General Manager, Swissair North America:* We feel that right now we have a tremendous fight on the North Atlantic that will last at least another year or two.

Stephen Aug: *(voice over)* Within the last year, American, Delta, and United have moved aggressively into the transatlantic market. One year ago tottering Pan Am and TWA were the main competition for the Europeans and the transatlantic market. Today, Delta replaces Pan Am as number two, American is three, and United is six. But suddenly the Americans say they're running into stiff resistance over further expansion.

Donald Carty, *Executive Vice President, American Airlines:* The European carriers have watched the stronger American carriers emerge as big, competititve airlines, not a substantially bigger competitive problem for them than Pan Am and perhaps TWA represented over the last decade, and they're concerned.

Stephen Aug: *(voice over)* Nor is that the only problem the European airlines are facing. Europe 1992 reforms are about to bring deregulation to the staid, noncompetitive, intra-European air travel market that some think could be as traumatic as deregulation was here.

Tim Pettee, *Analyst, Alliance Capital:* I think there will be a shakeout, a series of failures, Chapter 11's and eventually mergers among many of the carriers in Europe.

Stephen Aug: *(voice over)* The wave of mergers has already begun. Air France has gobbled up nearly all of its French competitors, while British Air is interested in taking over Holland's main airline KLM. In the meantime, all three have shown interest in taking over Sabena, Belgium's troubled state-owned carrier. Until recently national flag carriers have been sacred cows.

Donald Carty: I mean, we don't have flag chemical companies, but we do have flag airlines, and one of the things that will have to breakdown if the marketplace is really going to work internationally and the fittest survive is they'll have to be a disassociation, that'll have to be undone.

Stephen Aug: *(voice over)* There could be fallout on this side of the Atlantic. Fewer carriers could hurt the revenues of gateway airports like JFK, already wounded by the demise of Eastern, Pan Am, and the bankruptcy of TWA. The head of the agency running the airport says it will survive.

Richard Leone, *Chairman, New York Port Authority:* I think reports of JFK's demise are exaggerated, and as other airlines move out of gates—for example, this Lufthansa, Japan Air, Air France facility is being built on the old Eastern terminal site.

Stephen Aug: *(voice over)* There may also be opportunities for U.S. carriers to join multinational alliances.

Julius Maldutis, *Analyst, Salomon Brothers:* In order to be a global airline, you're going to have to join hands with one or two others, literally to span the globe.

Stephen Aug: *(voice over)* Maldutis helped engineer a partnership between Delta Airlines, Swissair, and Singapore Airlines that saves money by pooling marketing as well as sharing baggage and maintenance facilities. The partners say the passenger gets a seamless travel experience.

Peter Leuthi: The passenger can go from one carrier to the other with an easy timetable, with advantageous ground services.

Stephen Aug: *(voice over)* American, however, scoffs at such alliances as being high in publicity value and low in profits.

Donald Carty: We've seen a lot more talk about and announcements of global alliances than we've seen practical partnerships that generate incremental profit.

Stephen Aug: *(voice over)* In the meantime, nearly everyone agrees that international mergers and industry consolidation are inevitable. KLM already owns 20 percent of Northwest and, while American would not comment, it may be shopping for a European carrier.

Tim Pettee: They had been interested in British Caledonian going back a couple years, which British Airways bought, and American Airlines has expressed an interest in Sabena, the Belgian carrier.

Julius Maldutis: I believe that we will end up with perhaps seven or eight such global systems operating worldwide.

Forrest Sawyer, *ABC*: Well, what could block the prospect of international airlines mergers in this country at least is the federal law that forbids foreigners from owning a controlling interest in a U.S. airline, and then there is the matter of sovereign air space and national pride in the airline that flies one nation's flag. As government subsidies disappear, they're going to have to make money or go out of business. That wraps it up for this week. Whatever business you're in we hope the week ahead is a prosperous one. I'm Forrest Sawyer. On behalf of Stephen Aug and everyone here at *Business World*, thanks for being with us.

Announcer: *Business World* is a presentation of ABC News. More Americans get their news from ABC than any other source.

TRANSCRIPT 6

North American Free-Trade Agreement
from *Business World*, August 2, 1992

Announcer: From ABC News this is *Business World*. Now from New York, here's Stephen Aug.

Stephen Aug: It may be the weekend for most of us, but negotiators for the U.S., Mexico and Canada are hard at work in Washington, trying to hammer out the terms of the North American Free Trade Agreement. All parties are insisting that real progress is being made, but the closer they get to a finished product, the louder the cries are from critics, who claim free trade will be very expensive.

(voice over) It's easy to understand the economic motivation of the millions of Mexicans who try to cross the United States border each year. Workers at this Ford assembly plant in Mexico City earn as little as $65 a week. Counting fringe benefits, their counterparts in Detroit can make about 20 times more. General Dynamics pays these workers about 86 cents an hour for soldering — a job that pays about $8 in the U.S. It's no surprise that the prospect of a North American Free Trade Agreement has many in the U.S. worried, like the Economic Policy Institute, which has labor support.

Jeff Faux, *President, Economic Policy Institute*: You don't have to have a Ph.D. in economics to understand that if you have an opportunity as a manufacturer to go south of the border, and pay 10 cents in labor for every dollar that you're paying now, and still be able to sell those goods in the United States, you'd be a fool not to take advantage of it.

Stephen Aug: Some U.S. companies are already taking advantage of Mexican government incentives granted to foreigners by the Maquiladoras program. Falcon products makes these pedestal bases in Mexico, for furniture it makes in the U.S. While the company praises its Mexican employees for their ability to do difficult, heavy labor, Falcon says that work force may be ill-suited for other types of jobs.

Franklin Jacobs, *CEO, Falcon Products*: You have a tremendous amount of people who really don't know how to use a telephone, much less use a computer, and even though the state — the status of our educational system in this country may not be fabulous, it's still a heck of a lot better than it is in Mexico.

Stephen Aug: But critics say with all trade barriers dismantled, a broad range of jobs will move south, as it did under the Maquiladoras program.

Jeff Faux: Ten years ago, most of that business was in cut-and-sew apparel operations. Then they began to do more sophisticated labor. Then they began to do automobiles, machinery, consumer electronics. They're producing parts for American military jet planes in the Maquila.

Stephen Aug: But proponents of the treaty say lifting trade barriers will ultimately create more U.S. jobs, through increased exports. This study by the Institute for International Economics finds that the U.S. trade surplus with Mexico should reach $9 billion by 1995, creating a net gain of 130,000 U.S. jobs. But it also recommends that the government commit at least $900 million to retrain dislocated workers. NAFTA supporters also see increased trade as a way to boost the recession-ridden U.S. economy.

Paula Stern, *former Chairperson, U.S. Trade Committee:* The only growth in manufacturing jobs has been from exports to Japan, Germany, Mexico. Mexico is our fastest growing market, by the way.

Stephen Aug: And the agreement may mean increased trade south of the Mexican border.

Barbara Franklin, *Secretary of Commerce:* It further will serve to open a whole bunch of other Latin American countries that are literally right down the road from us —new markets, once again, for the U.S., where we have some newly democratized governments trying to privatize.

Stephen Aug: Both the U.S. and Mexican presidents are embracing NAFTA, and Democratic candidate Bill Clinton supports a qualified version.

Bill Clinton, *Democratic Presidential Candidate:* And I want to have an expanded trade with Mexico, but I want it to be fair to our workers.

Stephen Aug: But that may not be easy. Although Spain's integration into the European Community is often cited as a model, critics say it's a false analogy.

Jeff Faux: The Europeans have first-class training systems; they have national health care and health insurance, so that if you lose your job, you don't lose your health insurance.

Stephen Aug: There also is concern about Mexico's commitment to improve and enforce its lax environmental standards, to meet those of the United States. And there's opposition from the right. The U.S. Business and Industrial Council, a conservative business advocacy group, sees long-term problems with the agreement.

John Cregan, *U.S. Business and Industrial Council:* I think you're going to see Mexico turn into the Korea on our southern border—that is, export-oriented, fast-paced economic growth oriented, with exports—the majority of those exports headed toward the American market. And ergo, we will be running bigger and bigger trade deficits, and we will be losing more and more American jobs.

Stephen Aug: And even rules of origin provisions may not sufficiently protect against using Mexico as a platform for the U.S. market, if double-digit tariffs are reduced to two or three percent.

John Cregan: The rules of origin and the domestic content requirements are really rendered rather meaningless when the tariffs are brought down to such low levels that these foreign coporations are more than happy to pay the penalties.

Stephen Aug: U.S. presidential politics are playing a role in these talks, with both the Bush administration and the Mexicans anxious to wrap up the treaty before the election, while critics say, "What's the hurry?" After all, it took almost four years to hammer out the free trade agreement with Canada. That's it for this week. Whatever business you're in, we hope the week ahead is a prosperous one. I'm Stephen Aug, on behalf of everyone here at *Business World*, thanks for being with us.

Announcer: *Business World* is a presentation of ABC News. More Americans get their news from ABC than from any other source.

TRANSCRIPT 7

Corporate Quality in the U.S.

from *Business World*, November 15, 1987

Announcer: From ABC News, this is *Business World*, with Sander Vanocur, Stephen Aug, Dan Cordtz and Gordon Williams. Now from New York, here's Sander Vanocur.

Sander Vanocur: The merchandise trade deficits mean Americans are consuming more foreign-made goods while the rest of the world consumes fewer American-made goods. What happened to the days when buying a new car meant choosing between a Chevy and a Ford, not Toyota or Nissan? When television meant RCA or Zenith, not Sony or Panasonic? Business editor Stephen Aug reports it may take a look back to force a step ahead.

Singers: *(Chevrolet commercial)* . . .'57 Chevrolet trucks are here."

Stephen Aug: Remember when nearly everything you bought was made in the U.S.A.?

Singer: *(commercial)* I took my two hands and built an automobile.

Stephen Aug: And when "made in the USA" always meant quality.

Actor: *(RCA commercial)* Look at our new RCA Victor portable radio. Came through without a chip.

Stephen Aug: Goods that would last.

Actress: *(Westinghouse commercial)* You can be sure if it's Westinghouse.

Stephen Aug: And last.

Announcer: *(Timex commercial)* Timex. It takes a licking and keeps on ticking.

Stephen Aug: But today, many American goods are under attack on quality, and the number one example is the automobile. The latest automotive quality survey by the J.D. Powers Company shows Japanese firms way on top. To the biggest American auto firm, that's mostly a matter of expectation.

Robert Stempel, *President, General Motors:* If you look at the surveys that I think most generally are published, we're always surprised that, for instance, Cadillac and Mercedes and Jaguar don't have quite the high ratings of some of the Japanese products. And we think that's because the expectations for those cars are very high.

Stephen Aug: Stempel says the quality of American cars has improved so they're as good as those made elsewhere. Critics say that's not so.

Dan Howell, *Center for Auto Safety:* They have developed a lot of problem areas, particularly in American automatic overdrive transmissions. There are major engine problems, a lot of problems related to electronic components that control engine idle speed or cruise control or braking. These days it looks like there still is a significant gap between American car quality and some of the leading Japanese imports.

Stephen Aug: Yet not everybody agrees that the quality of American goods has fallen. Take a firm like Xerox. Nobody says they turn out shoddy goods. You find Xerox machines all over the world. And not only did they pioneer dry process copying, they continue to lead.

132

David T. Kearns, *Chairman, Xerox:* It's not so much a matter that United States slipped; it's that we lost track of what was going on all around the rest of the world, particularly out in the Pacific rim, because they went right by us, as far as the issue of reliability and quality.

Stephen Aug: And the reason?

David T. Kearns: We thought only about the domestic market and didn't really think about what it took to compete somewheres else.

Stephen Aug: At Corning Glass Company, they were nearly pushed out of the business of making support systems for automobile emission control. Corning invented that business when the clean air laws were passed.

James Houghton, *Chairman, Corning Glass:* We had the business, and all of a sudden the Japanese came in and were eating our lunch, they were taking it away from us. And our quality was just not good enough. And we came very close to going out of business. That may be a little over dramatic, but not too much. Well, the factory management there started putting in a total quality system, and today, four years later, we have the best quality in the world, we're shipping to Japan.

Stephen Aug: Four years ago at Eastman Kodak, 32% of their ectocolor photographic paper was defective. Now it's down to 2% and heading for zero. They solved that problem by teamwork, involving everybody in the department. In the department where Kodak makes film processing machinery, they've improved quality by expanding worker responsibility.

Colby Chandler, *Chairman, Eastman Kodak:* Each person along the line had the developing module as it was being assemble at their station for two hours, and so they were performing many functions in that two-hour interval. And the people are not robots because they are performing a variety of functions, and they seem to be as happy as I've ever seen any production person in my experience.

Stephen Aug: Levi Strauss and Company is one firm that never has lost its reputation anywhere in the world for producing quality goods. Just how do they do it?

Peter Thigpen, *Levi Strauss:* We don't build in obsolescence into our products. The longer our products last, interestingly enough, the more of them we sell.

Stephen Aug: Yet quality often takes a back seat to a quick fix on the bottom line because of pressure from Wall Street.

James Houghton: Because when you say "quality" to somebody from Wall Street, their eyes glaze over.

Stephen Aug: And senior management rewards only what happens in the short term.

David Nadler, *Quality Control Consultant:* I was recently working with a company, and in one of the plants they described how they have strict quality standards, but at the end of the quarter they typically end up shipping products that fall below those standards. And I asked them why, and they said, "Well, we have a quota to meet in terms of production."

Stephen Aug: And while at Japanese firms the cost of turning out shoddy goods runs about 3% of revenues, the cost at many American firms runs a huge 20% of revenues.

David Nadler: That is, what it costs them, to . . . for warranty costs, for repairs, for scrap, for returned goods, for the . . . having customer complaint departments, which is the cost of poor quality. If the customers were satisfied, they wouldn't call up and need help.

Stephen Aug: Many executives point out that the payoff from quality control is very quick. Once customers see quality, they start buying. On the other hand, you turn out shoddy goods, that customer's going to go elsewhere, whether it's another American firm or overseas. And that's one customer who could be gone for good. (Sandy?)

133

Sander Vanocur: That's it for this week. Whatever business you're in, we hope the week ahead is a prosperous one. I'm Sander Vanocur. On behalf of everyone here at *Business World*, thanks for being with us.

Announcer: *Business World* is a presentation of ABC News.

TRANSCRIPT 8

Chrysler/Ford Profits

from *Business World*, August 2, 1992

Announcer: From ABC News this is *Business World* from New York. Here's Stephen Aug.

Stephen Aug: After months of driving through red ink, two U.S. auto makers have found the black at the end of the tunnel. Ford posted a second quarter profit of $502 million. More surprisingly, Chrysler showed a second quarter profit of $178 million. Those figures raised the question, even if Detroit is leading, will the rest of the economy follow?

(voice over) The new Grand Cherokee Jeep has the starring role in Chrysler's surprisingly strong showing. It's impressing potential car buyers like Michael Towers.

Michael Towers, *Car Buyer:* Well, it's a unique design, I mean, plus it's American made. I know there's a Toyota Land Cruiser, and uh, you know, I mean, there are other —there's Ford products, but I've always liked the Jeep.

Farrell Furst, *Grand Cherokee Owner:* I think it's just the best. It rides great, it'scomfortable, has everything you want for.

Stephen Aug: *(voice over)* At Manhattan Jeep Eagle in New York City, they're having trouble keeping the Grand Cherokee in the showroom.

Jeff Monninger, *Manhattan Jeep Eagle:* The response has been a lot more and a lot greater than I had ever imagined, with the launch of this new vehicle. It really has just taken off tremendously, and right now, we're in a position where we can't get enough to sell.

Stephen Aug: *(voice over)* Led by the Grand Cherokee, Chrysler's line of lightweight trucks, including its minivan, have been a strong profit center for the company. Profit margins on truck sales are about twice those of car sales.

MaryAnn Keller, *Auto Analyst, Furman Selz:* For example, on the minivan, I estimate that Chrysler earns about $5,000 per minivan. On the Jeep—the new Grand Cherokee—probably $7,000 to $8,000 of profit.

Stephen Aug: *(voice over)* Like Chrysler, Ford also got a boost from its entry in the sports utility market. Despite the Grand Cherokee stealing some Ford Explorer sales, one Ford dealer even says he welcomes the new domestic competition.

Albert Vitarelli, *Manhattan Ford:* It's the Big Three again. You know, it's not so much the fact that we're facing off against the Japanese products all the time now; it's the fact that the three, the Big Three are competing for the marketplace, and they're coming out with some good stuff.

Stephen Aug: *(voice over)* Unlike American car makers, the Japanese have been forced to raise prices in the face of a strong yen against the dollar and higher borrowing costs at home, just to maintain profits. This has created a growing price disadvantage.

Joseph Phillippi, *Auto Analyst, Lehman Brothers:* We're talking about some very wide disparities in price between a Japanese vehicle and a domestic vehicle—the same size and model class, if you will.

134

Stephen Aug: *(voice over)* For example, a basic Honda Accord sedan with an automatic transmission lists for $14,560. A comparably equipped Saturn, made by General Motors, lists for only $11,620. As if to prove the point, Honda's Marysville, Ohio plant has announced plans to cut back production by about 10 percent, beginning in October.

Joseph Phillippi: We would expect that market share for the Japanese will probably fall again in July, as it has for about the past three or four months this year.

Stephen Aug: *(voice over)* And while overall consumer confidence is down, their cars are beginning to wear out.

Ann Knight *McFarland, Dewey and Company:* We've been through a long enough recession in the vehicle world that we've begun to see the build-up of real, honest-to-gosh need to replace used vehicles.

Stephen Aug: *(voice over)* Yet these positive trends may be of little benefit to General Motors. The struggling number one auto maker is expected to report only modest second quarter earnings this week.

MaryAnn Keller: Unfortunately, the more popular Chrysler and Ford cars and trucks have become, the more it has affected General Motors.

Stephen Aug: *(voice over)* And no one is betting that this latest uptick in Ford and Chrysler's earnings means the economy is about to go into high gear.

Dave McCammon, *Treasurer, Ford:* We are just growing at such a low rate that we can hardly believe it. This is unusual, right after a recession, to grow at this low a rate, and it's hard to see what's going to pull us out of it.

MaryAnn Keller: The Chrysler results should not be interpreted to mean that there's a strong recovery. Even in the worst depression, there's always something that sells very well.

Stephen Aug: And analyst MaryAnn Keller points out that this recovery—if that's what it is—is sluggish at best. In the first year of a typical recovery, auto sales are usually up by a million cars. This year, sales of both cars and light trucks combined are only expected to reach 400,000 above 1991. And that's it for this week. Whatever business you're in, we hope the week ahead is a prosperous one. I'm Stephen Aug. On behalf of everyone here at *Business World,* thanks for being with us.

Announcer: *Business World* is a presentation of ABC News. More Americans get their news from ABC than from any other source.

TRANSCRIPT 9

On The Road Again:
from *20/20,* January 25, 1991

Announcer: From ABC News—around the world and into your home—the stories that touch your life. This is *20/20* with Hugh Downs and Barbara Walters.

Harley-Davidsons—wheels of choice for hardcore bikers. More than a machine, a bit of Americana. It's not the same thing as the flag, but it's the same kind of idea. But a few years back, Harley almost went bankrupt. Foreign competition and shoddy workmanship, "the joke that was running around at that time was that sometimes you had to have two Harley-Davidsons, one of 'em as spare parts." Stone Phillips—with classic comeback; Harley-Davidsons, on the road again.

Barbara Walters: Here's a question for you. What travels in packs, breathes fire and not long ago was an endangered species? The answer, the Harley-Davidson motorcycle. To their fans, it's the king of the road, a bike for Americans built by Americans, but at the height of its popularity, the Harley almost suffered a wipe-out at the hand of Japanese competitors. Not so fast, said Harley. Stone Phillips has the story of the meanest bike on the highway.

Stone Phillips: *(voice over)* Open road, distant rumble. On a stretch like this in the 50's, Marlon Brando's *Wild One* introduced bad boys on bad bikes. Since then, countless wild angels and easy riders have criss-crossed our highways and movie screens, rebels in search of the real America. For hitting the freedom of the open road and blasting the establishment, there was one motorcycle of choice, nicknamed "the hog"—brand name, Harley-Davidson. Since 1954, the year of The Wild One, Harley has been the only motorcycle made in America. Hard-core bikers made solid customers. Someone's not likely to change brands if he's tattoed the logo on his arm. Loyalty like that made Harley an American institution.

Biker: It's not the same thing as the flag, but it's the same kind of idea. It's a concept.

Stone Phillips: *(voice over)* To its owners, Harley is not just transportation, but a work of patriotic American art. (on camera) If each is a work of art, as many Harley owners believe, then this is the original masterpiece, the first Harley-Davidson ever built, the original "hog," on display here at the company's corporate headquarters in Milwaukee. It was introduced in 1903, the same year Henry Ford built his Model A, the year the Wright brothers got a machine of their own up and flying. Now, compared to those achievements, mounting a motor on what is basically a bicycle frame may seem like a relatively minor practical advance in the science of transportation, but William Harley and his partners, the Davidson brothers, were never aiming for practicality. They were building machines designed for pleasure; and though, through the years, Harleys developed a reputation for being loud and spilling oil and breaking down, customers became hooked on the Harley mystique and the company became convinced that no matter how unreliable the product was, the flaws would always be forgiven because they were made in America, they were classics, they were Harley-Davidsons.

(voice over) But this classic motorcycle became a classic case of American industry left in the dark by Japanese competition. The ghost in the machine came back to haunt Harley. By the mid-1970's, half the bikes coming off the main assembly line in York, Pennsylvania were missing parts. Quality, quite literally, was a joke. Joe Smith now manages the York plant.

Joesph Smith, *Plant Manager:* The joke that was running around at that time was that sometimes you had to have two Harley-Davidsons, one as spare parts, in order to keep one on the road.

Stone Phillips: *(voice over)* At the time, Harley was owned by the American machine and Foundry Company, AMF. To cash in on a 70's cycle boom, they triple production and quality went bust. Harleys with faulty parts and chronic oil leaks dripped onto the market like blood in the water and the competition moved in for the kill. Japanese motorcycles in the same class offered more power, higher quality at lower cost. Japanese companies had established a beachhead in the 60's with smaller bikes, referred to in Harley circles as "Jap crap," but they were selling to people who'd never bought bikes before. Jerry Wilke is Harley's Vice President for Marketing.

Jerry Wilke, *Vice President, Sales and Marketing:* Honda came on the scene and they came up with a very, very effective marketing campaign, "You meet the nicest people on a Honda."

Stone Phillips:: Implicit in that ad was the message that the people who ride Harleys aren't necessarily the kind of people you want to meet.

Jerry Wilke: It was because of some of the movies, you know, the Marlon Brando movies and all the other things, that created what was the motorcycling image at that time.

Stone Phillips: *(voice over)* Japanese marketers set out to change that image, not only going after the first-time riders Harley ignored, but a clean-cut, upscale market likely intimidated by Harley's tougher image and bigger bikes. It worked. As the overall number of motorcycle riders went up, Harley's share went down. In 1973, Harley had 77 percent of the market for heavyweight bikes, the only kind it makes. By the start of the 80's, Harley's share had plunged to under 31 percent and many Harley workers were out in the cold.

Shirley Messinger, *Motorcycle Assembler:* We went through a lot of lay-offs and a lot of bad times. I was laid off for 17 months, came back and production was slow at the time, but we kept running.

Stone Phillips: *(voice over)* Just barely. Harley's comeback from near collapse, says one analyst, is an amazing Rust Belt success story. It began in 1981 when Willie G. Davidson and 12 other Harley executives raised $80 million in loans to buy back the company his grandfather had started—desperate gamble, high stakes.

Willie G. Davidson, *Vice President of Styling:* A lot of us went through some rough, sleepless nights and also some tough years as far as economics and our investments and whether this piece of history would still be here or not today is a big question.

Stone Phillips: *(voice over)* Davidson is head of styling and many credit his designs with keeping Harley going while others got the financial act in order. The new focus was keyed to staying close to the customer and the product. Many Harley executives ride to work, even during a Milwaukee winter. Riding and talking with customers established what they wanted—designs based on classic Harley styling, a product which was reliable. To give them that, Harley executives implemented, in their own plant, quality production techniques they'd picked up on a tour through Honda—employee involvement in decisions, smaller inventories and overall concentration on quality.

Jerry Wilke: A lot of those are Japanese techniques and we have stolen shamelessly in many of these cases.

Stone Phillips: *(voice over)* While they stole from the Japanese, Harley got U.S. tariff protection, four years of stiff import taxes on heavy Japanese motorcycles. Still, the financial outlook was bleak. Lenders were getting cold feet. Harley lawyers were working on bankruptcy papers.

Jerry Wilke: You can't imagine how tough the tough times were and you can't imagine how close this company came to going upside down. And I mean it, it came within days of having the company go out of business in the mid-80's.

Stone Phillips: *(voice over)* A last-minute reprieve from a finance company headed by a Harley buff and a $20 million stock offering kept the motor running and better than it had before. Harley ads stressed overcoming past defects, but there was still the image problem. *(on camera)* Here in Sarasota, Florida, we found the perfect example of what has happened since Harley sent its image in for repairs. They didn't go for the tune-up, they went for major overhaul and what they delivered to Harley buyers accustomed to greasy bike shops is one heavy-duty shock.

(voice over) The juke box in the corner of the Sarasota dealership features a classic biker beat, but the atmosphere here is upscale boutique. Part of the company's new success—licensing

the old name. Products from helmets to leather jackets to silk underwear bear the logo, beef up profits, attract new Harley clientele.

Rick Rossiter, *Harley-Davidson Dealer:* Their image in the past didn't appeal to that type cutsomer and that type customer didn't go into the Harley shop. That type customer likes to come into this store.

Stone Phillips: This store does not look like a Harley-Davidson dealership. It looks like Bloomingdale's.

Rick Rossiter: Thank you. We worked very hard to get it that way. I think Harley really is looking for the middle- and upper-income people who can afford a $10,000 motorcycle.

Stone Phillips: *(voice over)* This gang, for example, includes an insurance executive, two school teachers and the CEO of a large Florida banking consortium. The new marketing tactics put a different breed of customer on hogback and why not? Malcolm Forbes and other friends in high places had made Harley respectable. Great free publicity against the competition. Kawasaki Vice President for Marketing, Bob Moffit.

Robert M. Moffit, *Vice President, Marketing, Kawasaki:* The fact that Harley-Davidson and motorcycles are part of the lives of a lot of well-known, respected people, whether you're talking about the Malcolm Forbes of the world or the Jay Lenos or the Mickey Rourkes or any number of people from a variety of backgrounds. Harley has played that marketing card very, very effectively.

Stone Phillips: *(voice over)* Indeed, classic Harleys are now for sale in pricey stores like The Sharper Image, evidence that all the changes came together for Harley. Latest figures show them dominating the market with 62 percent of big bike sales, up from 28 percent in 1985. During the same time, Honda's share was steadily shrinking. But as impressive as Harley's comeback is, there's a catch. As their market share grew, overall U.S. sales dipped, so Milwaukee now targets overseas. Harley's found its largest export market in Japan. Japanese Harley buyers are lured by the same pitch Harley gives in the U.S.-When you buy a Harley, you buy heritage, you buy adventure, you buy the lure of the open road.

Hugh Downs: Stone is on assignment right now in Los Angeles, but Stone, you know, that kind of comeback is the sort of story we'd love to be able to report about other U.S. businesses. Why can't we?

Stone Phillips: Hugh, the message from Harley executives has been, "If we can do it, you can do it," but this is a company that's had aces up its sleeve. For instance, right here in Hollywood, celebrities have posed for free with their motorcycles for Harley's brochures and promotional literature. Malcolm Forbes and Elizabeth Taylor—the sight of those two riding around on a Harley probably did as much as anything to change the image and it didn't cost the company a penny. So they got smart, but they also got lucky with some free publicity that other companies just can't count on.

Hugh Downs: Curiously, my son is a Harley owner and my father was also.

Barbara Walters: But I remember when you were off on your motorcycle and did yourself a little damage.

Hugh Downs: Yes but you know that was not a Harley though.

Barbara Walters: I see, it was your fault.

Hugh Downs: Right.

Barbara Walters: Well, I'm Barbara Walters.

Hugh Downs: And I'm Hugh Downs.

Barbara Walters: And for everyone here at *20/20,* thank you for watching. Good night.

Announcer: *20/20* is a presentation of ABC News. More Americans get their news from ABC than any other source.

TRANSCRIPT 10

Flexibility of Companies to Workers' Family Care Needs
from *World News Tonight,* November 27, 1989

Announcer: From ABC, this is *World News Tonight* with Peter Jennings.

Diane Sawyer: Tonight on the American Agenda, balancing work and family. It used to be that companies would tell their employees when you come to work leave your family problems at home. But that was before the homemakers started taking other jobs. Now that the baby boom is over and skilled workers are in such demand, women are entering the work force in record numbers. As Rebecca Chase tells us, that has forced some companies to change the way they do business.

Rebecca Chase: *(office)* It is a quiet but dramatic revolution, jobs are being redefined, traditional career paths replaced, company benefits restructured. For corporate America these changes are business decisions.

Peter Pesce, *Vice President, Arthur Anderson:* We have a basic philosophy that says we want to hire the best and the brightest.

Dennis Kessler, *Fel-Pro:* And I mean recruit and keep good people, we have to fill their needs.

Arnold Hiatt, *Stride Rite:* It's not diluting our earnings, it's improving our earnings.

Rebecca Chase: *(Employee with son)*: Every survey shows that child care is the number one problem for employees. Four thousand employers now offer some form of assistance. *(Time Building)* the newest example, five New York based companies pay for a trained worker to go to an employee's home when a child is sick or the normal child care arrangement breaks down. *(Home worker arrival)* It is an answer to one of working parents' biggest worries. With his son provided for, Peter Gordon, a Home Box Office emplyee is able to go to work.

Shelly Fischel, *Vice President, HBO:* If the person who can then come into work is someone we would otherwise replace with a temporary, it is actually saving us money.

Rebecca Chase: *(Day care scene)*: For two decades, Stride Rite shoe company's on-site day-care has helped the shoe manufacturer attract better employees, reduce turnover and improve productivity. *(Office building)* So how Stride Rite is breaking new ground. In January, it will open a second day-care center for the elderly relatives of employees.

Arnold Hiatt, *Stride Rite:* We're in the business of looking for return on our investments and we find that that kind, what is considered essential investment, has a very large economic return.

Rebecca Chase: *(Senior citizens)*: Helping employees care for their elderly relatives is the latest company benefit. With the population aging, an increasing number of workers are faced with that responsibility. Like IBM marketing manager, Jim Askew, whose mother-in-law was frail and living alone in New Jersey. With the help of IBM's Elder Care Information and Referral Service, Askew moved her to a retirement village near his home in Atlanta.

139

W.E. Burdick, *Vice President, IBM:* Employees who are preoccupied or frustrated with this issue aren't going to be applying their time and focus to their job and their career as they and we would like.

Rebecca Chase: The most progressive companies are offering employees flexibility. *(Office)* Flexible hours, leaves, and part-time work. Arthur Anderson, the accounting firm, goes even further. It allows employees to work part-time, yet stay on track to become partners in the company. *(Carey at work)* Three days a week, Carey Brown is an audit manager. *(Carey at home)* The rest of the week she is a full-time mother.

Peter Pesce, *Arthur Anderson:* We found that if we weren't willing to address these issues, we then made a decision that says we will take the risk of losing top talent in this firm.

Rebecca Chase: Time magazine offers another innovative alternative. *(Mary Jane at desk)* Mary Jane Berrien works Monday, Tuesday, and Wednesday. *(Susan at desk)* Susan Ostreich works Wednesday, Thursday, and Friday. They are advertising account managers who share one job. This allows them to give both their clients and children the attention they need. *(Women with kids)*.

Susan Geisenheimer, *Vice President, Time Magazine:* I'm thinking ahead to, if things are going to get tough in terms of the labor market, I want to make sure that we're the kind of company that people are always going to want to work for.

Rebecca Chase: The number of family friendly companies is growing, but most employees do not enjoy any of these benefits. Companies say they are too expensive or not equitable becasue they cannot be used by everyone or simply that businesses should not be involved in family matters. But increasingly, these views are considered shortsighted. *(Various home scenes)* The new demographics are a reality and companies that do not help employees balance work and family will simply lose out to those that do. Rebecca Chase, ABC News, Atlanta.

Peter Jennings: That's our report on the World News Tonight. We'll be here again tomorrow. I'm Peter Jennings. Good night from Czechoslovakia.

Announcer: This has been a presentation of ABC News where more Americans get their news than from any other source.

TRANSCRIPT 11

Computers and Consumers: User-Friendly or User-Surly?
from *Business World*, April 29, 1990

Announcer: From ABC News, this is *Business World* with Sander Vanocur and Stephen Aug. Now from New York, here's Sander Vanocur.

Sander Vanocur: The New York Futures markets were shut down for most of Friday. Why? Computer failure. One day this winter half the nation's long-distance calls didn't get completed. Again, computer failure. Those are giant systems, but the same problems on a smaller scale are every day events. After all, there are an estimated 43 million personal computers in use in the U.S. It's an industry that has revolutionized our lives, improving productivity, employing directly or indirectly hundreds of thousands—one of the few industries in which the U.S. still leads the world. But what about the other side of this $35 billion a year business, with its jargon of disk crashes and format failures, where computers seem more surly than friendly, and where sometimes we're made to feel that when systems fail, the fault lies with the users, not the makers. Just ask Mitch Kapor, the founder of spreadsheet maker Lotus.

Mitch Kapor, *CEO, On Technology:* So there's this conspiracy of silence, that, that, PC's, despite all the wonderful things that they can do as word processors or spreadsheets, databases, for the average person are still frustratingly difficult to use, and that's the secret shame of the industry.

Sander Vanocur: *(voice over)* That view is echoed even by some of the advocates of the newest technologies, like consultant Patricia Seybold.

Patricia Seybold, *President, Office Computing Group:* Most of us are sitting here thinking, "I must be stupid. There's something wrong with me because I can't figure out how to make this machine work," or "I can't figure out how to use this particular software package," and the fact of the matter is it's the programs that are stupid and the people selling the systems that are stupid by not making them more obvious and easy to use and intuitive.

Sander Vanocur: *(voice over)* PC Labs spends $3 million a year to test the performance of hardware and software products, and even with its expertise, can't always get products to run.

Fred Davis, *Director, PC Labs:* I get frustrated trying to get things to work, plug it together, you'd like to think that it was a plug and play technology. I think consumers are somewhat up the creek without a paddle. I hate to say it and I wish it weren't so.

Sander Vanocur: *(voice over)* Still, Davis reports only product performance, not necessarily how long it takes to get it out of the box and get it running right. Just this week, Vaugh at IBM recalled its $500 add-in card becasue it was destroying data. Why such a sorry state of affairs? It's part hardware, part software.

Bill Machrone, *Editor-in-Chief, "PC" Magazine:* The biggest overall issue is compatibility. People buy a product and assume that it will work with the other products that they already own. It's not necessarily so.

Sander Vanocur: *(voice over)* At Boston-based Stone and Webster Engineering, PC's from several makers are used for everything from engineering design to travel planning, and document storage. And the purchase price for the firm's 1,200 PC's was only the beginning.

Glen Orenstein, *Stone and Webster Engineering:* We see annual costs ranging anywhere, depending on the study that you read, anywhere from $6,000 up to $18,000 per year per microcomputer.

Sander Vanocur: *(voice over)* Corporations already spend 56 cents of their software dollars on training and support, only 44 cents to actually acquire it.

Charmaine Proskauer, *Bank of Boston:* Probably spend 80 percent of the time training people on 20 percent of the function of the software package, and if we can get 80 percent of the people using it, then we think we've done our job.

Sander Vanocur: *(voice over)* For smalll businesses, like New York's Washington Street Cafe Caterers, computer failure can be more than costly. When a computer holding the plans for a sit-down dinner failed, it was a recipe for disaster.

Ronnie Davis, *Washington Street Cafe:* We did the party by picking up the telephone and saying, "Pardon me, I hate to bother you with this, but my computer is down, and we just can't recall what time we're serving the salmon," and when the client said to me, "We're serving Chateaubrien," we realized right then that we were in big trouble.

Sander Vanocur: *(voice over)* Now, besides putting it on his Compaq, Davis keeps a printed back-up copy of everything. Software manuals all have instructions for making backup copies of your programs, and advise backing up data as well. Could it be because they expect failures? Those problems aren't limited to IBM-compatible computers. California theatrical producer Chuck Eisler was using an Apple Macintosh when a 24-page proposal went to "Data Heaven."

Chuck Eisler, *Theatrical Producer:* There were moments of thinking about maybe going back to longhand and typewriters and calculating machines, you know, that there was some saving grace in those after all.

Sander Vanocur: *(voice over)* And there's a psychic cost to computerization, especially for someone who is forced into a computing environment. Before computerization, this is how insurance benefits analysts at one company pictured themselves, and this is how computerization changed the picture. John Hancock found its hands full when it tried to computer train its entire insurance sales force.

Ken Shackett, *John Hancock Financial Services:* Hardware failures, unplugged systems, you name it, and the whole gamut, and I don't think we were really quite prepared for the deluge of calls and problems that were going to crop up.

Sander Vanocur: That's it for this week. Whatever business you're in, we hope the week ahead is a prosperous one. I'm Sander Vanocur, on behalf of everyone here at *Business World*, thanks for being with us.

Announcer: This has been a presentation of ABC News where more Americans get their news from any other source.

TAPESCRIPT 12

Sharing Sweet Success
from *20/20*, May 22, 1992

Announcer: From ABC News, around the world and into your home–The stories that touch your life with Hugh Downs and Barbara Walters. This is *20/20*.
How would you like to have bosses like these? If they get a raise, you get one. No wonder employees love them, but so does Wall Street. And this is a shareholders meeting (singing on video). Who are these guys? Ben & Jerry: Getting rich selling super rich ice cream, but always spreading the wealth. Their golden rule? How much do we benefit the community and how much money do we make. Bob Brown with Ben & Jerry. Sharing Sweet Success!

Hugh Downs: How much money do you make, compared to your boss? In recent months, there have been numerous stories highlighting the sometimes enormous gap between executives and workers on the line and other stories about workers laid off, considered disposable in a sluggish economy. Well, tonight, Bob Brown introduces us to a couple of extremely successful businessmen who take a totally different approach. They spread the wealth and they take care of their employees and the community.

(voice over) In fact, at Ben & Jerry's Ice Cream, everybody's troubles just seem to melt away.

Bob Brown: *(voice over)* Amid the thaw of a Vermont spring, we're about to enter the world of a company that links the pay of the highest executive to the lowest worker, an environmentally sound, politically correct corporation that nevertheless makes profits a robber baron would envy. If it weren't for the butterfat, it would be hard to find anything that sounds sinful about Ben & Jerry's. Constant streams of children flow up and down the slanted walkway into this ice cream factory near the woods, young Hansels and Gretels who, instead of being incarcerated by a wicked witch, are indoctrinated, as they stuff themselves, by signs of the social mission that defines what Ben Cohen and Jerry Greenfield—two guys who grew up in the 60's—want their company to stand for.

Jerry Greenfield, *Co-Founder:* Our social mission here is central to all the stuff we do, so that we try to have a social component that's involved in, you know, pretty much all the activities of the company.

Ben Cohen, *Co-Founder:* And then, we have our two-part bottom line that measures both things—how much do we benefit the community and how much money do we make.

Bob Brown: *(voice over)* Even though they don't look the part, they are shrewd businessmen who have managed to live up to both their ideals and their stockholders. They make what's called "super premium" ice cream, with high butterfat content and less air in the mixture. Ben & Jerry's has 38 percent of that super premium market, second only to Pillsbury's Haagen Dazs and well ahead of Kraft Foods' Frusen Gladje. They seem to have an uncanny instinct for off-beat concoctions that boost sales. Their most recent flavor, Chocolate Chip Cookie Dough, is now their most successful. And sensitive to diet research that shows fat is bad, they have now gone full throttle into frozen yogurt products. The bottom line—this year, Ben & Jerry's will, for the first time, top the $100 million mark in sales, double the sales figure of only four years ago. Marie DeLucia follows franchised industries as a Senior Vice President of Tucker Anthony.

Marie DeLucia, *Senior Vice President, Tucker Anthony:* Today, as we enter the '90s, coming out of the sort of greed of the '80s, I believe some investors are going to be willing to pay maybe an even higher premium for companies like Ben & Jerry's that pay attention to the bottom line for their employees and for their shareholders, but also for others.

Bob Brown: *(voice over)* How do they mix ice cream with a social mission? Example: They buy their main ingredient, the milk, from a Vermont dairy cooperative because they believe in supporting small farms. Example: These brownies going into Ben & Jerry's Chocolate Fudge Brownie ice cream come from the Greystone Bakery in Yonkers, which reinvests its profits into providing jobs and training for the homeless. Example: Ben & Jerry's hires its own workers from every spectrum of the community. The company provides this on-site child care center at its Waterbury plant, which employes around 350 people. And as for the stockholders, well, a Ben & Jerry's stockholder meeting is something to behold.

Marie DeLucia: It was like nothing that I had ever seen before. I went to the one last year in late June and it was part of a festival weekend that Ben & Jerry's was hosting. It was under a tent. The Chairman of the Board and many of the executives were in Bermuda shorts and t-shirts.

Ben Cohen: We shall now proceed / with voting on the election of directors / which is item one on the notice of the meeting.

Marie DeLucia: Ben sings the opening, you know, all the legalese.

Bob Brown: *(voice over)* You won't find many people complaining about that irreverence.

Two Shareholders: We second that emotion.

Bob Brown: *(voice over)* Last year, the value of Ben & Jerry's stock increased 150 percent and the company reported record earnings of $3.7 million. These people, on the other hand, probably couldn't care less about how the stock performs. They're just here to see how the ice cream is made.

Factory Tour Guide: We put in 400 pounds of the finest Dutch chocolate into that blender.

Bob Brown: *(voice over)* Last year, a quarter of a million people made this pilgrimage to Ben & Jerry's main ice cream factory in Waterbury, Vermont. It is the most popular tourist attraction in the state. If there's one area where Ben & Jerry's is strictly business, it is an obsession with quality control. It's a daily routine, here in the factory, to slice open pints of ice cream to make sure the ingredients and chunky things, for which Ben & Jerry are most famous, are distributed evenly.

Ben Cohen: I'm looking for cherry chunks.

Bob Brown: *(voice over)* When he is testing the quality of the products, Ben, as Chairman of the Board, tends to lose his sense of humor. We found him in his office, cutting up some new frozen yogurt pops with cherries in them. He was laughing, but he was not happy.

Ben Cohen: There's several little bits of cherries in here, but there's no real cherry chunks and what we talk about this in the industry is that we have a "loss of fruit identity." And you know, you don't really get like a burst of cherry flavor out of a little fleck like that, do you?

Bob Brown: I guess not.

Ben Cohen: No.—useless.

Bob Brown: *(voice over)* Ben sent the pops right back to the Research and Development division, which six weeks later, was still trying to figure out how to make the chunks larger.

Ben Cohen: As Jerry and I have always said, it's easy to make it lousy, it's hard to make it right.

Bob Brown: *(voice over)* While Ben has been most involved in corporate affairs, Jerry is a kind of company cheerleader–the guy who goes out on the road to talk with distributors and franchise owners. Ben & Jerry's has virtually no national TV advertising budget. The company likes to go one-on-one with the customers.

Jerry Greenfield: We tend to spend our money, you know, marketing the ice cream, but more through promotions or community events or things that tend to be more fun.

Ben Cohen: You know, we have these scoop trucks that drive around different cities in the country and just give out free samples all day, every day of the year.

Bob Brown: *(voice over)* Because of the enormous growth that has occurred over the last 10 years, Ben & Jerry have turned over most of the responsibility for daily business operations to a senior management team that also stays aligned with the values on which the company was founded. But anyone who takes a managerial job here has to know one thing up front. The highest paid executive at Ben & Jerry's can earn no more than seven times the salary of the lowest paid worker.

Ben Cohen: What they do is who we are, is what we make and how can you possibly justify somebody making a million or more dollars a year when their line-level worker can't make enough to afford a house?

Bob Brown: *(voice over)* The issue is one that's been prominent lately because of the inflated salaries of corporate chief executives who, according to recent statistics, take home, on average, 70 times more than their lowest paid workers. What the seven-to-one ratio means here is that no executive at Ben & Jerry's is currently earning more than $100,000 a year. *(interviewing):* And that's something that's important to you and that you do think about?

1st Employee: If they want to make more, we have to get a raise, too, so they can make more.

2nd Employee: It makes you feel valued. You know, just because my range is, you know, not way at the top, I'm still important, even though I'm in there. And I'm treated like, you know, I'm important.

Bob Brown: *(voice over)* Do these guys do anything wrong? As a matter of fact, yes. In 1990, Ben & Jerry's was nailed with more than $30,000 in fines for creating excessive levels of ice cream waste around their plant. *(interviewing)* Now all these plants are being grown from ice cream—

Ben Cohen: Ice cream waste.

Bob Brown:—ice cream waste?

(voice over) They did build this experimental greenhouse overlooking the plant to recycle a small perentage of the waste, but they have a long way to go. And they've even agreed in advance to pay more fines if they violate waste limits. They do try. Another of their solutions for dealing with this slop was much less traditional. They found out that ice cream waste is okay for pigs to eat. The problem was there were no pig farmers in the area, so Ben & Jerry set up a farmer with his own herd of swine and voila. As their company song points out, a Ben & Jerry's franchise is a Ben & Jerry's franchise, no matter where you find it.

Singers: There ain't no Haagen, there ain't no Dazs / There ain't no Frusen, there ain't no Gladje / There ain't nobody named Steve at Steve's / But there's two real guys at Ben & Jerry's.

Ben Cohen: We believe that we've come upon a way of doing business that integrates the concerns of the community with making a profit. Take a look. If you like what you see, do it. If you don't, don't.

Barbara Walters: Chocolate Chip Cookie Dough? Why didn't you bring back samples for your friends?

Bob Brown: Oh, you'd need to have an oxygen mask standing by if you try a whole pint.

Barbara Walters: How do they still manage to do business when more and more people want low-fat or non-fat frozen desserts?

Bob Brown: Well, they've gone heavily into frozen yogurt products now. That's one of their biggest pushes. They both publicly consume pints and pints of frozen yogurt. It has, they say, about one-eighth the calories of that super premium ice cream. That's not to say it doesn't still have a lot of calories.

Barbara Walters: Yeah. It's so strange that they went to Vermont. How did they get started in the first place and why would you go to the coldest place?

Bob Brown: They'd known each other since the seventh grade. They tried a series of odd jobs and neither one of them really made it, so they said, "Well, let's open a homemade ice cream shop." They looked for college towns with no homemade ice cream stores and the only one they could find was in Vermont, which is cold most of the year. So they went to a converted gas station there, opened an ice cream store and the rest is history.

Barbara Walters: Well, they picked a beautiful state and it shows if you make a good product, they'll even eat it where it's cold. Next time, bring samples.

Bob Brown: I will.

Hugh Downs: I've gained a pound and a half just listening to you, Bob. That's *20/20* for tonight. We thank you for being with us.

Barbara Walters: Just in time, we have to say we're in touch so you be in touch, I'm Barbara Walters.

Hugh Downs: And I'm Hugh Downs.

Barbara Walters: And we wish you a good holiday weekend, goodnight.

Announcer: *20/20* is a presentation of ABC News. More Americans get there news from ABC News than from any other source.
